THE COGNITIVE BEHAVIORAL THERAPY
WORKBOOK FOR PANIC ATTACKS

THE COGNITIVE BEHAVIORAL THERAPY WORKBOOK FOR PANIC ATTACKS

BY ELENA WELSH, PHD

ROCKRIDGE
PRESS

Interior and Cover Designer: Michael Cook
Art Manager: Sue Smith
Editor: Nora Spiegel
Production Manager: Oriana Siska
Production Editor: Melissa Edeburn
Cover Illustration: © vlastas/Shutterstock
Author Photo: Courtesy of Birdie Thompson

ISBN: Print 978-1-64152-604-3 | eBook 978-1-64152-605-0

Contents

Dedicated to everyone who has anxiety
but shows up for what matters to them anyway.

Welcome

Anxiety is the most common mental health challenge people experience. Everyone experiences some anxiety from time to time, and up to 40 million adults in the United States meet the criteria for an anxiety disorder. For some people, anxiety doesn't have much of an impact, but for others it can be crippling. Because it is so common, almost everyone I've worked with in therapy experiences some anxiety, even if it isn't their primary reason for seeking help.

Many people with anxiety also experience panic attacks, which are the focus of this workbook. Panic attacks can be a symptom of another type of anxiety disorder, or they can be a result of their own disorder—meaning panic attacks occur unexpectedly without any other manifestations of anxiety and without a specific cue or trigger. Some people might experience one or more panic attacks during times of heightened stress, only to have those symptoms decline when their stress level returns to normal. I fall into this last group.

I had my first panic attack during a time of high stress and uncertainty, when I was applying to PhD programs in psychology. Even though I had enough clinical training to know what was happening to me when the panic hit, it was still incredibly scary to feel like I had no control over my physiological responses. For me this was an isolated incident, but for many people a first panic attack can spiral into regular attacks, intense fear of experiencing panic, and eventually full panic disorder. If you experience this, I am happy you picked up this workbook. Together, we will work through these challenges so that you come out the other side with fewer panic symptoms and stronger coping skills.

This workbook is designed to home in on panic symptoms and reduce them as rapidly as possible. All the strategies used in the book are evidence-based, meaning they've been scientifically tested and proven to work. If you commit to using these practices, you will see results. Finally, if you are diagnosed with some other type of anxiety disorder—like Generalized Anxiety Disorder (GAD), Obsessive Compulsive Disorder (OCD), or social phobia—and have panic attacks as part of a cluster of other symptoms, you'll need to use this workbook in conjunction with treatment for your larger issue.

How to Use This Book

Use this workbook in whatever way you find most helpful. You might work your way through the book from beginning to end. However, you don't have to read the chapters in order; you may prefer to begin with whichever section makes the most sense for you, depending on how you're feeling and what you are struggling with most right now. For example, if your biggest concern at the moment is that fear of having a panic attack is causing you to avoid going out in public, you can begin with chapter 5, "Your Behavior and Fear-Based Avoidance." If the physical sensations of panic are the most distressing aspect of your panic attack, you could start with chapter 3, "Your Body and Physiological Signs of Panic." If your tendency to exaggerate and catastrophize things in your mind is the main driver of your symptoms, you could turn to chapter 4, "Your Brain and Panicky Thoughts."

Wherever you begin, know that you will experience the most success and long-term progress once you cover all the sections in the workbook. Panic can show up anytime and anywhere, so you should cover all the bases. Once you have completed the workbook in its entirety, return to and review any sections that address issues you're still struggling with.

Chapter 1 gives you an overview of panic, and chapter 2 gives you a foundational under-standing of the cognitive behavioral therapy (CBT) strategies that will be used throughout the workbook. If you are unfamiliar with CBT, you may find it helpful to review this sec-tion first, however you proceed. Subsequent chapters address the specific areas in which your panic symptoms are likely manifesting: your body (physiological symptoms), your thoughts, and your behavior.

CHAPTER ONE:

Understanding Panic

Panic attacks are very common; nearly a quarter of all adults will experience at least one panic attack in their lifetime. If you're reading this book, you're probably one of those people. Even when panic attacks are isolated experiences, the effects can be very disruptive and upsetting. If you experience panic attacks more frequently, the impact is even more devastating and often comes with other unpleasant consequences, including public embarrassment, increased general anxiety, and physical side effects, such as gastrointestinal issues.

A panic attack is a sudden rush of fear and physical discomfort that usually peaks within minutes. This rush distinguishes panic from other kinds of anxiety symptoms. Panic attacks can occur when you're feeling anxious, but they can also strike without warning when you are feeling calm or happy. Because so many physical symptoms are associated with panic, it isn't always immediately apparent that you are experiencing an anxiety reaction. In fact, many people mistake panic attacks for heart attacks or other serious health events and go to the emergency room or urgent care. That reaction makes sense because the physical symptoms associated with panic attacks are similar to those experienced in cardiac events, including heart rate changes, sweating, trembling, or shaking, along with a choking sensation, chest pain, shortness of breath, nausea, chills or heat sensations, numbness or tingling sensations, headaches, and dizziness. I've worked with clients who did not believe they were experiencing panic until multiple urgent care or emergency room visits had confirmed there were no other physical concerns.

The physical sensations of panic can be accompanied by anxious thoughts, such as fears of losing control or dying, feeling as if you're going crazy, or feeling detached from yourself or reality. However, especially at first, some people experience only the physical components of panic, which can make it hard to determine whether the experience is related to anxiety. A complicating factor is that panic sensations can arise from medical conditions, such as hyperthyroidism or asthma. *Therefore, it is always advised that you seek medical attention when initially experiencing panic attacks*. Once you have been medically cleared, you will likely have to repeatedly remind yourself that your symptoms stem from panic, because in the midst of subsequent attacks your mind may convince you that there's something physically wrong.

Technically speaking, a panic attack occurs when you experience at least four of the symptoms just described. Given the wide range of possible symptoms, a panic attack for one person could look and feel very different than it would for someone else. Moreover, your own panic attacks may not always feel the same. One panic attack may have you sweating, shaking, feeling like you are choking, and feeling nauseated, whereas another attack may involve chest pain, numbness, dizziness, and an intense fear that something is very wrong physically.

If you've experienced one or more attacks, you may have heard or read about *panic disorder*. Panic disorder is diagnosed when you experience recurrent and unexpected panic attacks (i.e., panic attacks with no obvious trigger). Additionally, you may experience persistent worry about having additional panic attacks and even change your behavior to avoid them, for example, by ceasing activities that raise your heart rate or staying away from public places. This book will help you reduce the frequency and intensity of panic attacks, while also helping you become more comfortable and less fearful when panic does strike.

Panic vs. Anxiety

Panic is distinct from other forms of anxiety in a number of ways. Whereas most forms of anxiety are accompanied by some distinct physical sensations, such as muscle tension or increased heart rate, physiological sensations dominate the panic experience and are the defining characteristic of a panic attack. These physical experiences themselves eventually become the object of fear in panic disorders. In other words, with panic disorder, your greatest source of anxiety becomes the question of when and where panic will strike next. Panic is not secondary to your fear of some other thing, like heights or social situations.

Panic is also distinct from general anxiety due to its abrupt onset and short duration. A panic attack is characterized by a sudden surge of discomfort that typically reaches a peak within a few minutes, whereas in other forms of anxiety the physical sensations are typically lower grade, and anxious feelings and thoughts are more chronic. Although you will likely experience residual anxious thoughts following an attack, your panic symptoms typically will last fewer than 15 minutes.

Another defining feature of panic is the catastrophic thinking that often accompanies the physiological sensations. For example, during a panic attack someone might start to think, "I'm going to die," because they interpret their lightheadedness and dizziness as signs of a terminal brain tumor or stroke. I worked with a young woman whose strong choking sensations always made her think she might choke to death, thus exacerbating her panic experience. Others might think they're having a heart attack because they suddenly experience chest pain and numbness. In fact, it has been estimated that nearly 25 percent of people who visit the emergency room with chest pains are actually experiencing a panic attack.

Regardless of what you tell yourself is happening when panic strikes, even in the absence of catastrophic thinking, panic symptoms make you feel as though you have no control over your body. The physical sensations often feel uncontrollable, and you are unable to simply "calm down." Unfortunately, the more you focus on your physiological sensations and catastrophize their meaning, the more adrenaline or stress hormones your body will release. You get caught in a panic feedback loop, with the physical and cognitive symptoms increasing and prolonging each other. It can be a very scary experience.

Cued vs. Uncued Panic Attacks

Another key distinction between panic disorder and other types of anxiety is the experience that the panic attack is uncued, meaning that it comes out of nowhere, with no clear trigger or reason for occurring. This experience differs from that of a person who has panic attacks only in response to a particular feared situation. For instance, a person with social anxiety, who often has panic attacks in response to public speaking or meeting new people, understands that the panic attacks are a result of social anxiety and predictably occur when the social fears are triggered. Similarly, someone who is afraid of needles may predictably experience a panic attack every time they get a shot or have blood drawn. For individuals with posttraumatic stress disorder, a panic experience may sometimes *feel* unexpected, but most often the experience is cued or triggered by a reminder of the traumatic experience, which may not readily be recalled due to memory repression. In hindsight, trauma survivors are often able to identify what triggered their panic experience.

In contrast, someone who is experiencing panic disorder may feel that some panic attacks come out of nowhere. They may even feel happy or calm when panic strikes, which can make the experience all the more jarring and frightening. Even if some panic attacks are predictable, perhaps following a particularly stressful day at work, those with panic disorder are likely left with the uneasy sense that panic could strike at any moment. Thus, many people who experience uncued panic attacks will develop persistent worries about unexpected panic attacks.

Fear Itself

The hallmark feature of panic disorder is that your fear of future panic attacks, rather than some other fear—say, fear of heights—becomes your primary concern. That is, your anxious thoughts and distorted thinking begin to focus on the experience of the panic attack *itself*. As your fear of having a panic attack increasingly dominates your thinking, you may begin to change your behavior to avoid the experience. In the same way that someone with social anxiety might try to avoid public speaking, someone who is experiencing panic disorder symptoms might begin to avoid situations in which panic might occur. This strategy might mean avoiding exercise because you worry that the experience of being short of breath will trigger an attack, or it might mean avoiding public situations in which you would feel embarrassed about people seeing you have a panic attack.

As your fears and worries about future attacks grow, you may also become more likely to misinterpret other physical cues, such as dizziness or shortness of breath, as a sign of an impending attack. The resulting spike in your stress hormones further increases the chances that you will experience an attack. You may also develop fears that your attacks are signs of an underlying illness, such as a heart problem or seizure disorder, or that you are "going crazy" or "losing your mind." With each panic attack, your mind may support your fears that you are dying or losing control of yourself. Your panic-related catastrophic thoughts may intensify with each attack, thus amplifying the physical sensations, which could lead you to experience more frequent and intense attacks.

How Is Panic Affecting Your Life?

Let's take some time now to examine how your panic attacks and other panic symptoms are impacting your life. Like other mental health difficulties, panic can increasingly affect your life. How has panic impacted your overall sense of life satisfaction or feelings of safety or control? For many people, the experience of panic attacks, and the accompanying worry about future attacks, can be so unpleasant and discouraging that they may cause associated feelings of hopelessness, sadness, or loss of control. If you struggle with depression or other forms of anxiety, panic symptoms could contribute to a worsening of those symptoms.

Another question to consider is how panic may be affecting your relationships. Think back to the quality of your relationships prior to the onset of your panic symptoms. Have you begun to avoid someone to prevent them from seeing you have a panic attack? Have you started avoiding events you used to enjoy, like dinner parties, out of fear of another attack? As the list of situations to avoid grows longer, many people become increasingly isolated from important relationships. Even if you're not *intentionally* avoiding people, your avoidance of certain places and situations likely affects your contact with others. For instance, are you less likely to see a friend because you no longer feel comfortable taking walks together? Are you less likely to say yes to social invitations because of fears related to your panic experience?

Another important area to consider is your work life. Have you missed more work or school lately? Perhaps you've missed important obligations due to frequent visits to urgent care for panic-related symptoms. Are you increasingly distracted by worries about future attacks and how to avoid them? Being more distracted and less present could potentially impact your productivity or motivation.

Panic can also negatively affect the routines of daily life. Do you now avoid ordinary activities in which you once engaged? Have you stopped exercising? Do you now avoid stairs? In the beginning, these changes in your routine may seem harmless and may even help you feel that you have more control over your symptoms. However, over time, the more people and situations you avoid, the more likely you are negatively impacting your overall health and well-being.

The following exercise will help you determine just how much your life is affected by your panic experiences.

Self-Assessment: How Are Your Fears of Panic Impacting You?

Take a moment to think about the issues discussed on page 5, and indicate the degree to which panic has impacted the following areas of your life.

MY RELATIONSHIPS

0	1	2	3	4
Not at all	A little bit	Somewhat	Extremely	

MY WORK OR SCHOOL

0	1	2	3	4
Not at all	A little bit	Somewhat	Extremely	

MY MOOD

0	1	2	3	4
Not at all	A little bit	Somewhat	Extremely	

MY DAILY ACTIVITIES

0	1	2	3	4
Not at all	A little bit	Somewhat	Extremely	

You may be surprised to note that panic is focused primarily in one area of your life, or that it is impacting a great deal of your life. Like other anxiety disorders, the effects of panic can creep in gradually, and you may not have realized to what extent in your daily life.

The Cognitive Behavioral Method

Thoughts, emotions, and behaviors are interconnected and influence one another. This insight is the core of cognitive behavioral therapy (CBT), which focuses on intervening to change one of these three domains (e.g., behavior) to change the other two. CBT strategies help you change the way you think and what you do so that you can feel better.

Take thoughts. Often it's your thoughts about life events, rather than the events, that cause you distress. If you interpret your shortness of breath as the result of having just run up some stairs, you won't feel distressed. But if you interpret your shortness of breath as a sign that you're about to have a panic attack, you would likely feel upset. In this case, it is not the shortness of breath that's causing you to be upset, it's the way you are thinking about it.

Using CBT strategies to change the way we think, especially if our thinking has become particularly negative or catastrophic, has proven to be highly effective in improving many mental health problems, including anxiety.

Some newer cognitive behavioral therapies that have proven highly effective in treating anxiety and panic include acceptance and commitment therapy (ACT), dialectical behavioral therapy (DBT), and mindfulness, so we will use strategies from these therapies throughout the workbook. These therapies place a strong emphasis on what is important to you and your lived experiences. Specifically, ACT helps us think flexibly, tolerate uncomfortable thoughts and emotions, and take actions in our lives that are consistent with what we value. DBT and mindfulness will help us stay in the present moment and regulate our emotions, calming fears that demand our attention and control our behavior.

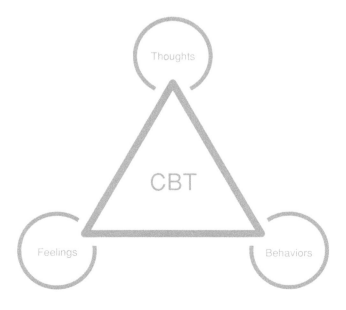

Panic Disorder Assessment

Complete the following questions:

1. Do you experience panic attacks?

   Yes / No

A panic attack is an abrupt surge of intense fear or discomfort that usually reaches a peak within minutes. During a panic attack you will experience some of the sensations listed below.

Consider your most recent panic attack and place a check mark next to each symptom you experienced:

- ❑ Palpitations, pounding heart, or accelerated heart rate
- ❑ Sweating
- ❑ Trembling or shaking
- ❑ Sensations of shortness of breath or smothering
- ❑ Feelings of choking
- ❑ Chest pain or discomfort
- ❑ Nausea or abdominal distress
- ❑ Feeling dizzy, unsteady, lightheaded, or faint
- ❑ Chills or heat sensations
- ❑ Paresthesia (numbness or tingling sensations)
- ❑ Derealization (feelings of unreality) or depersonalization (being detached from yourself)
- ❑ Fear of losing control or "going crazy"
- ❑ Fear of dying

Total number of panic symptoms: _____
(four or more symptoms constitute a panic attack)

2. Do at least some of your panic attacks come "out of the blue" or feel unexpected?

   Yes / No

3. After a panic attack, did you experience a period of time of at least a month during which you either:

> Had persistent worries about having future panic attacks or had fears about what the attacks mean (i.e., that you are sick or losing control)
>
> **OR**
>
> Changed your behavior, such as not doing something in order to avoid having the attacks or to avoid being embarrassed by them

Yes / No

Interpretation:

- If you answered yes to questions 1, 2, and 3, you are likely experiencing panic disorder.

- If you answered yes to question 1, but no to questions 2 and 3, you are likely experiencing panic attacks stemming from a specific fear, such as social situations, needles, or heights.

- If you answered yes to any two of the three questions, it is unclear if you are experiencing a panic disorder, but you are experiencing some of the symptoms related to panic disorder.

- If you selected fewer than four panic sensations in question 1, you are likely experiencing limited symptom panic attacks.

For a conclusive diagnosis, please see a mental health professional. You can use your answers from this list to inform your work with a mental health professional and to track your healing.

Key Takeaways

After reading this chapter, you should have a good understanding of panic attacks and the key characteristics of panic disorder. Additionally, you should have an initial understanding about whether or not you are experiencing panic attacks or panic disorder. You have learned that:

- A panic attack is an abrupt surge of intense discomfort that typically reaches a peak within minutes.

- Panic attacks can come out of the blue.

- Panic disorder is characterized by recurrent and unexpected panic attacks, persistent worry about further attacks, and changes in behavior to avoid them.

- Cognitive behavioral therapies have proven effective in reducing the frequency of panic attacks and in relieving some of the negative consequences of the attacks, such as associated worry or behavior changes.

CHAPTER TWO:

Your CBT Toolbox

As we saw in chapter 1, cognitive behavioral therapy (CBT) is a broad term that includes a large set of scientifically tested strategies that work across a wide array of symptoms. CBT strategies are extremely effective in treating anxiety, and panic disorder specifically. The cognitive behavioral model is based on the premise that our thoughts, behaviors, and emotions are interconnected and influence one another. Therefore, each intervention strategy will intentionally target change in one of these areas, with the goal that change in one area will impact the entire interconnected system.

At times, these strategies may feel contradictory. For instance, at one point you might track your panic attacks in order to detect patterns or triggers and reduce their frequency, whereas at another point you may be working on strategies to become more accepting of and comfortable with the panic sensations. Your CBT toolbox will include a number of strategies to help you tackle your difficulty with panic attacks from many different angles. With practice, you will figure out which tools work best for you.

The Best Strategies for Panic

There are many different techniques that have been shown to reduce anxiety and panic. Some of the core CBT interventions that seem to work best include:

- **RELAXATION STRATEGIES** to help you relax and learn how to breathe in ways that calm you down.

- **COGNITIVE STRATEGIES** that help you catch and correct any faulty or distorted thought patterns.

- **MINDFULNESS STRATEGIES** to help you focus on the present moment, as opposed to your fears about what is coming next.

- **ACCEPTANCE STRATEGIES** that help increase your tolerance for uncomfortable feelings, so your panic and anxiety don't derail your day-to-day life.

- **EXPOSURE STRATEGIES** to help you face and experience the very things you are afraid of in order to, paradoxically, reduce your fears. There are three main types of exposure techniques:

  * *Imaginal exposure* involves imagining, in great detail, experiencing your feared events or situations.
  * *In vivo exposure* involves putting yourself in real life situations that are scary for you.
  * *Interoceptive exposure* involves exposure to the feelings of anxiety and panic in your body.

Exposure techniques are highly effective in reducing panic symptoms. In many ways exposure is the easiest treatment protocol to develop and follow, because it's so straightforward. However, this type of treatment plan is often easier said (or written) than done. Because of how scary some exposure techniques can be, it's important to incorporate other therapeutic strategies and concepts in order to help you develop the motivation and skills to follow through with an exposure protocol.

I had a therapy client named Josh who initially developed panic attacks in response to his fear of heights, but this quickly spiraled into full-blown panic disorder because his fears about when his next attack would strike increased his anxiety and led to more attacks. Within the first few sessions, he articulated a hierarchy of his feared situations and sensations, and we developed a plan to begin doing exposures.

Based on our initial plan, Josh would have moved through his feared situations at a relatively quick pace, potentially concluding therapy after only a few months. However, when the day came to engage in the first interoceptive exposure exercise, during which he was going to self-induce feelings of shortness of breath, he understandably came up with every excuse in the book. He felt he was too tired to take on the task that day and had other things he wanted to discuss in therapy first. However, he was sure he would be ready to try the exercise the following week.

As you can imagine, with the next week came new reasons why it was not the right time to try the exercise. We had to take a step back and work on other skills and exercises before he felt ready to proceed. We worked on developing his basic skills related to physical and mental relaxation so he could begin from a relative state of calm. When he became clearer about his reasons for wanting to reduce his panic symptoms, and had more awareness of the ways in which his anxiety was causing him to compromise his core values, he had more motivation and better skills with which to tackle the difficult exposure experiences. In this case, it was the combination of exposure techniques with other strategies, like mindfulness and acceptance, that worked to relieve his panic symptoms. We will discuss these strategies in more depth, starting with mindfulness techniques.

Mindfulness

Mindfulness practices are being increasingly incorporated into psychotherapeutic techniques and appear to be highly effective. Rooted in ancient Eastern techniques, mindfulness strategies have been shown to reduce a wide range of psychological symptoms and disorders, including anxiety, depression, and substance abuse. Mindfulness is often confused with meditation, and although there is some overlap, mindfulness is more of an attitude and daily practice as opposed to a singular activity. Researchers who study the efficacy of mindfulness strategies have focused on isolating the following five facets: *observing, describing, acting with awareness, nonreactivity,* and *nonjudging.*

Mindfulness can be described as the capacity to maintain awareness of, and a sense of openness to, what is happening around us in the here and now. In contrast to being preoccupied with negative thoughts about our past or worries about our future, mindfulness encourages us to fully attend to the present moment and to view ourselves and the world from a nonjudgmental, compassionate stance. This begins with simply *observing* and *describing* what you see, hear, and feel in any situation. With this increased *awareness,* you are then able to *act* with more intention.

For example, if you are hungry and tired, you may be more likely to feel short-tempered and snap at a friend or loved one. With increased awareness of these initial physical states of hunger and tiredness, you may be more likely to grab a quick bite or take a few deep breaths, which in turn may prevent you from becoming short-tempered in the first place. For many of my clients with panic, the ability to remain attuned to their physical and emotional sensations helps reduce the feeling that panic comes out of nowhere. When they learned to notice the subtle shifts in their body and thought patterns that preceded panic, they were more able to proactively address them as opposed to spiraling into a state of panic.

The *nonreactive* aspect of mindfulness means that you can learn to observe difficult thoughts such as "I am scared I will have a panic attack if I go on the hike" without getting emotionally swept up in the experience. You can observe that you are experiencing a fearful thought without necessarily having an intense emotional reaction that accompanies that thought. The *nonjudgmental* aspect of mindfulness encourages us to stop using labels like "good" and "bad" to define our experiences, but rather to simply be and observe. *Nonjudgment* was a critical skill for Josh, as we saw earlier. When he became more accepting and less judgmental of the physiological anxiety experience, he had less fear about it happening, which in turn decreased the severity of his physiological panic response.

As people develop mindfulness skills, their ability to cope with difficult thoughts and emotions improves, and additionally there is often a decrease in maladaptive behaviors and their consequences. For instance, if someone cannot tolerate feeling lonely, they might engage in a host of behaviors to avoid the feeling, such as excessively drinking alcohol or becoming involved in an unhealthy relationship. The more we can remain open and curious about what we're experiencing, instead of judging it, the more rooted we are in the present moment. When we inhabit the present moment, we are less susceptible to being carried away by the emotional stories we tell about our experiences. As it turns out, this makes experiences like loneliness and fear less painful.

Mindfulness techniques are particularly effective in reducing anxiety due to the emphasis on maintaining a present moment "here-and-now" focus. Because anxiety is often anticipatory in nature, when we remain focused on the present we are less likely to develop psychological distress related to events or scenarios that have not even happened yet. The next time you begin to feel anxious, start by gently pulling your attention back to the present moment. The mnemonic STOP is one tool to help you do this.

S—Stop.

T—Take a deep breath.

O—Observe: What do you see? Notice how your feet feel on the ground. Notice the tempo of your breath. Observe and label your thoughts without necessarily becoming attached to them. Notice the temperature.

P—Proceed.

Mindfulness can also take you on a walk, and many people find this to be a very useful tool.

Mindful Walking

This walking meditation can be done anywhere, but may be more pleasant to do in relative solitude or outside in nature.

1. Begin with noticing your posture. Try to stand as straight as possible, without feeling tight or clenched.
2. Take a moment to roll your shoulders back in order to loosen them.
3. Take a long deep breath in and exhale slowly.
4. As you begin to walk, notice each movement that you make with your feet. Notice your foot lift, your foot hovering above the ground, and finally the placement of your foot on the ground.
5. Say (or think) "lift," "carry," "place," as you make each movement.
6. Continue walking slowly in this manner for a few minutes.
7. When you are ready to turn your attention away from your movement, shift your awareness to your surroundings. What do you see? Hear? Smell? Actively label what you observe, either in your mind or out loud.

With its focus on the present moment, mindfulness may be a well-used tool in your CBT toolbox. You can bring your attention to a single moment—to a single breath—with a thoughtful pause, and with movement; you have it available to you at all times.

BENEFITS OF MINDFULNESS

Mindfulness skills typically encompass the following activities and attitudes: observing, describing, acting with awareness, nonreactivity, and nonjudgment. Although these skills may come more naturally to some people, they can also be learned, which is the goal of mindfulness-based therapeutic strategies. Scientific studies of mindfulness-based treatments have found that they're effective in reducing anxiety, stress, and depression, and even in reducing future instances of depression. Research also suggests that mindfulness skills can enhance the effectiveness of other therapeutic interventions. Attending to, observing, and describing your emotional experiences can help facilitate the therapeutic process to work more effectively.

One component of mindfulness—the ability to maintain focused attention in the present moment—has been found to directly correlate with reductions in anxiety and worry. Similarly, the ability to label feelings with words (*describing*) is related to lower levels of physical arousal during anxiety. The skill of *nonreactivity,* which is the ability to let feelings come and go without getting drawn in by them, has been shown to lower overall distress, as well as to reduce the distress that comes from anxious thinking. Like any skill, the development of mindfulness comes through sustained practice. You can think of mindfulness as a muscle that grows stronger with regular use. Begin with a small moment of mindfulness, even if it's as simple as taking a minute to focus on the inhalation and exhalation of your breathing. Mindfulness is a skill that anyone can cultivate, and, like anything else, the more time you spend practicing it, the stronger those essential coping skills will become.

Acceptance

Acceptance is a core concept in acceptance and commitment therapy (ACT). In ACT, *acceptance* is defined as being open to the full range of human experience, which includes unpleasant emotions and undesirable experiences like a panic attack. When we close ourselves off to unpleasant feelings and experiences, we end up missing out on opportunities for growth, connection, and fun. Furthermore, the ways that we avoid unpleasant emotions, like drinking alcohol or binge eating to escape feeling sad, often cause further problems.

This doesn't mean that we just give up or resign ourselves to having panic attacks, but rather that we accept that pain will be an inevitable part of our journey toward living a full life. More importantly, acceptance teaches us that even our most difficult emotions and sensations don't have to stop us from living the lives we want. Once you've practiced acceptance for a while, you'll come to more deeply understand that the problem is not the panic itself, but your struggle *against* the panic that's causing you the most problems. Your constant worry and anticipation of an attack, the myriad ways you have changed your life to avoid triggering panic—this is actually the source of most of your distress. Although they can feel extremely uncomfortable and scary, panic attacks themselves are of short duration and don't do lasting harm. If you can accept and become willing to fully experience the panic sensations, you are, paradoxically, taking a critical first step in reducing your panic attacks.

The tug-of-war metaphor is often used in ACT to illustrate how acceptance leads to relief from symptoms. Imagine you're playing tug-of-war with a monster who represents all your fears, sadness, and anxiety. You believe that if you win, the monster will go away forever, but if the monster wins, your fears may overwhelm you. Imagine pulling the rope back and forth repeatedly. Deadlocked in the struggle with your own thoughts and emotions, you eventually become exhausted, because it's an unwinnable game. The "monster" will never entirely go away, because worry, distress, and pain are unavoidable parts of human life.

Even more importantly, as you're frantically pulling the rope, all the things that are important to you, like your family and friends and job, are going on without you. The endless tug-of-war is taking up energy and attention that you'd probably rather spend on other things.

So what's the solution? In the end, it's a simple one: Just drop the rope. Yes, that may mean that the monster can now wander around freely, and for a while you may experience even more anxious thoughts and sensations. But the truth about the monster is that it can't really harm you, and giving up your struggle means that you'll be more engaged with the things that matter to you and that make your life worthwhile.

Because the concept of acceptance can be difficult to understand in an abstract way, the following two exercises will help you find ways to apply it in your life.

Acceptance vs. Avoidance

This first exercise explores the ways you think about your unpleasant experiences. If you imagine a continuum that represents all the different ways we can approach our life experiences, acceptance and avoidance are on opposite ends of that spectrum. To help you identify the areas in which you can work on bringing in more acceptance, start by identifying the experiences you are trying to avoid.

THOUGHTS: _____

_____

_____

_____

FEELINGS/EMOTIONS: _____

_____

_____

_____

PHYSICAL SENSATIONS: _____

_____

_____

_____

What do you do to avoid or escape these experiences? Take your time and be as specific as possible.

_____

_____

_____

_____

_____

_____

_____

Have any of your avoidance strategies caused you problems, or caused you to miss out on something important? How so?

_____

_____

_____

_____

_____

_____

_____

_____

With these notes in hand, the next exercise moves beyond the page and will allow you to practice acceptance. You may also spot some elements of mindfulness as you read the instructions on page 23.

Acceptance of Negative Emotions: Inviting Discomfort

This is an experiential exercise. You may want to read through the text below once in its entirety. To begin the exercise, read the text a second time, pausing after a few lines to close your eyes and experience what the text is talking about. Don't force it. Let whatever comes up, come up.

> Which emotion do you have the hardest time with? Is it loneliness? Sadness? Fear? Close your eyes and imagine inviting that emotion to come. Think of something that makes you feel that uncomfortable emotion. If the emotion doesn't come, that is okay, too. What is important is that you are willing to feel it.

> If the difficult emotion shows up for you, observe what you are *feeling*. What physical sensations do you have? Where are you holding tension? Take a deep breath and visualize the breath filling the parts of you that are tense.

> What are your *thoughts* surrounding this emotion? Resistance? Fear? Something else? Imagine what it would feel like to accept these thoughts for what they are: just thoughts, and nothing more.

> See if you can sit with everything that comes up for you. Work on accepting it fully, without judgment. Accept it into your mind, heart, and body. When you notice an urge to avoid or escape the sensations, notice and accept these feelings, as well.

Mindfulness and acceptance are critical tools you can develop to deal with the feelings that a panic attack induces. Next we'll turn our attention to the C in CBT: cognitive interventions.

Cognitive Interventions

Because our thoughts influence our emotions, errors in our thinking patterns can cause unnecessary emotional pain. In particular, the physical sensation of panic is often exacerbated by the kind of faulty thinking we're all prone to at times. The common thinking errors we all share—such as overestimating threats—are called *cognitive distortions,* and are the cause of a lot of unnecessary distress. Cognitive interventions target this faulty thinking and help replace it with more productive thoughts and beliefs.

We all make thinking errors sometimes—like thinking a friend is mad at us because she didn't return a text, when in fact she'd left her phone at home and didn't see it. There are particular types of thinking errors that are common in people dealing with anxiety. One of these is a tendency to *catastrophize*, or focus on the worst possible outcome. Examples of catastrophizing include thinking that the tight sensation in your chest means you're having a heart attack, or assuming you will get fired after making a mistake at work. Other cognitive tendencies that are common with anxiety include:

> **JUMPING TO CONCLUSIONS** or predicting the future (e.g., assuming that you will have a panic attack at an important social event).
>
> **TUNNEL VISION,** which occurs when you focus on threat information and ignore signs of safety (e.g., focusing on the information you read on the Internet that suggested that lightheadedness may be a sign of a brain tumor, while not considering the fact that you stood up quickly or had not been drinking enough water).
>
> **EMOTIONAL REASONING,** which occurs when you take your emotions as *de facto* logic, such as assuming that because you feel anxious, something bad is likely to occur (e.g., I feel anxious, therefore there must be something wrong).
>
> **OVERGENERALIZATION,** which occurs when you take a single example or instance of something and assume it will continue to happen (e.g., if you have a panic attack while on a date, you assume you will panic every time you go out with someone).

The first step in reducing the emotional burden of faulty thinking is catching it when it happens. This is why it can be helpful to know the names of common thinking errors (such as catastrophizing), so you can label and categorize your distortions as you catch them. After learning about cognitive distortions, most people are able to immediately recognize a few that they commonly engage in. If that's the case for you, start there and see if you can catch yourself in the act.

If you're still having difficulty catching your own thinking errors, work backward and start with the distressing emotion. When you get upset or particularly anxious, try to identify some of the thoughts you had right before you felt upset. It can also help to write your thoughts down in quotes, or as close to verbatim as possible, so you can analyze your thinking to detect any distortions.

Once you've identified a thinking error, you can begin to develop a more balanced viewpoint by asking yourself questions about how realistic the thought is, pondering alternative explanations that are more balanced than your distorted thinking, or even testing your cognitive distortions against reality (we'll examine these strategies in later chapters). In general, cognitive interventions will help encourage you to be less extreme and reactive in your thought processes and will give you more control over how much you allow your thoughts to influence your emotions and behaviors.

The strategies discussed thus far—mindfulness, acceptance, and cognitive interventions to target distorted thinking—have focused on thoughts and feelings. CBT also addresses *behaviors*, and that's where we turn next.

Graduated Exposure

Experiencing panic attacks, and developing fears about having more of them, will most likely cause you to avoid things, situations, and people you either associate with panic, or believe would make having a panic attack even worse. For instance, you may avoid exercise out of fear that it will induce panic sensations, or you may stop going to the movies because it would be hard to get out of a theater quickly in the event that you panic. It is natural to avoid things that make you anxious; the problem is that avoidance only provides short-term relief, and in the long run it intensifies your fear reactions. If you experience relief after avoiding exercise, for example, your brain strengthens the association between fear and exercising.

On the other hand, if you approach the situation you are anxious about, you give yourself the chance to have a corrective learning experience and allow your brain to learn a new association. Let's take the example of Yuki, who was scared to have a panic attack in the movie theater because she believed it would be too hard to get out of the theater to safety. To reduce her anxiety, she started avoiding going to the movies. As a result, her fear of the theater and similar public venues, like concert halls, continued to grow. It seemed like no big deal to skip movies at first, but eventually, there were events that Yuki was really sad to miss, like the time a big group went to the movies for Yuki's best friend's birthday, or the Saturday when her young niece asked her to take her to a matinee.

If Yuki were willing to experience her fear of theaters long enough to actually get to the movies, she'd probably have a good time and her brain would have a new association to make between movies and fun, or between movies and quality time with a loved one. Even if Yuki did end up having a panic attack, by facing her fear she might also learn that she underestimated her coping skills and could get herself outside to fresh air easily, without anyone really noticing. Such an experience could also lessen Yuki's fear association, based on the new information she'd learned about her ability to handle panic attacks.

Facing our fears is no small feat. Because of how scary it can be to approach the things we want to avoid, it is advised to pace yourself and start small. Remember that every journey starts with a single step. You can begin by facing a very small fear situation and working your way up. Later chapters of this book will walk you through the process in more detail, but the general concept is that you start by thinking about everything you are anxious about or want to avoid, and develop a list of these fears. For individuals experiencing panic disorder, it is important to include situations you are afraid of, like the movies or driving alone at night, as well as sensations that you associate with panic, like feeling short of breath or dizzy (termed *in vivo* and *interoceptive* exposure, respectively). You will begin with the situations and sensations with the lowest fear ratings and work your way up.

Before you begin, you may want to spend some time learning ways to relax effectively, or working on developing mindfulness skills. These tools will help you tackle your fear hierarchy, but don't wait too long. Procrastination is a friend of avoidance. You can always continue to develop other coping tools while you begin to approach the situations you are anxious about.

Next Steps

If you have experienced a panic attack, you know how powerful and all-consuming it can feel. Although there is no quick fix to conquering such a mighty fear, the tools in this book are driven by theory, have undergone rigorous scientific inquiry, and have helped thousands of people experience relief from anxiety and panic. The tools won't work unless you do; here are some strategies that will optimize your recovery journey:

Set aside dedicated time. Plan to spend some time daily, or at least a few times a week, to do the reading and exercises in this workbook.

Get organized. Keep an additional notebook to use for further homework or to journal about your experiences.

Ask for help. Ask a trusted friend or colleague to help you stay on track and to help with certain exercises. Seek the advice or consultation of a mental health professional to help you get started or get you back on track if you get stuck.

Key Takeaways

This chapter provided an overview of the therapeutic approaches and tools that have been found to be effective in reducing panic symptoms, and that we will continue to use throughout the workbook. Specifically, we covered:

- The techniques that have been found to be particularly helpful with panic disorder, including mindfulness, acceptance, cognitive strategies to address common distortions, and exposure.

- The therapeutic benefits of mindfulness and acceptance strategies, including increased comfort with difficult emotions and an ability to remain in the present moment.

- Common thinking errors, including catastrophizing, jumping to conclusions, tunnel vision, emotional reasoning, and overgeneralization. Becoming aware of our thought distortions can help us regain a more balanced perspective.

- Graduated exposure, another effective tool in reducing panic attacks, wherein we face our fears in order to provide ourselves with opportunities for learning new associations.

CHAPTER THREE:

Your Body and Physiological Signs of Panic

As we've talked about, the physiological symptoms of panic—from sweating, to dizziness, to heart palpitations, to nausea—are the core features of panic attacks, and are by far the most distressing part of the panic experience for most people. The sensations are overwhelming and often come out of nowhere. They can be so distressing that people often mistake their first panic attack for some catastrophic physiological event, like a heart attack. If you are reading this book, you likely know how distressing and scary the experience is. The good news is that these acute bodily sensations are generally of short duration. They do not and cannot last forever. If you learn to ride them out, rather than resisting them or letting your fear of the sensations ratchet up your panic further, you can shorten the length of the panic experience even more. Ultimately, with practice, it's possible to dramatically reduce or even end the distressing physiological symptoms of panic.

Panic and the Body

The physiological surge of fear you experience during a panic attack is your body's normal response to danger—it's just happening at the wrong time. During a panic attack, your body is responding to danger that is not really there. When we detect danger (or think we do), our brain sends a signal to the *autonomic nervous system,* which is composed of two parts: the *sympathetic nervous system* and the *parasympathetic nervous system.* The immediate fear reaction, which is called the *fight-or-flight response,* occurs when the sympathetic nervous system is activated. This process is intended to keep us safe by getting the body ready to "fight" or "flee," and it does so almost instantaneously. If you encountered a bear while you were alone in the woods, the fight-or-flight response would be completely warranted and might save your life.

When the sympathetic nervous system is activated, your body releases stress hormones such as adrenaline and cortisol. Your heart rate increases as your body prepares for action by increasing the speed of blood flow in order to improve the oxygen delivery your body needs for energy. Additionally, there are changes in blood flow to more effectively prepare you for action by concentrating blood where it is needed most, such as in large muscles, and by reducing blood flow where you need it less, like in the extremities. This is why you may experience temperature changes or weakness in your hands or feet during panic. This temporarily reduced blood supply to your brain is responsible for sensations of dizziness or blurred vision.

Additionally, because your body needs more oxygen for the fight-or-flight response, it is normal for your breathing to become more rapid. Sweat glands are activated in order to cool the body down, which is why sweating is a common panic sensation. Further-more, because energy is redirected from the digestive system, you may experience nausea or diarrhea, as well as decreased salivation, which leads to sensations of dry mouth and may contribute to feelings of choking or suffocating. As your muscles prepare for action, you may experience muscle tension, or even trembling and shaking. These are all normal physical reactions to fear. Remember, these physical changes in your body are protective, because they are designed to keep us safe. Although they may feel extremely uncomfort-able, they are not harmful.

Unfortunately, when your mind tricks you into thinking these sensations are harmful—thinking, "Oh my God, I'm having a heart attack"—the intensity of the experience will only increase. This happens because your anxious thoughts communicate danger to your body, thus prolonging and intensifying your body's attempts to protect you. If you can increase your level of tolerance for these uncomfortable sensations, you will be able to help your body recognize that there is no actual danger, thus slowing, or even reversing, the fight-or-flight reaction.

Even if it feels like it might, the panic experience physiologically can't go on forever, and it won't ever reach physically damaging levels—that's just not how those bodily responses work. The rush of all those stress hormones is a discrete physical event with a beginning, middle, and end. Your body will fairly quickly reregulate itself and bring you back down toward your baseline—so long as you don't prolong the attack by catastrophizing it in your mind, which will continue to send your body threat signals. The more you're able to remind yourself that you are not in actual danger, the more quickly you will be able to bring your parasympathetic nervous system on board. If you are in the midst of panic, but say or think, "I am okay," or "This is my body's normal reaction to fear," while taking slow, deep breaths, you are speaking directly to your parasympathetic nervous system. When the parasympathetic nervous system is activated, hormones that induce feelings of calm and relaxation are released, countering the effects of the sympathetic nervous system.

Even after your body has stopped responding to the perceived threat, some of the stress hormones take a while to fully disintegrate. This is why you may still feel "on edge" for a while after the full panic experience has subsided. Other people describe feeling exhausted after experiencing a panic attack. This is because the fight-or-flight response activates your whole body and takes a lot of energy.

The daily stressors in our modern lives, like traffic, relationship problems, and work deadlines, lead to an increased release of stress hormones such as adrenaline and cortisol. This is why you're more likely to experience a panic attack when you are under stress. Your body is already primed for the fight-or-flight response, so it will react to perceived danger more easily and intensely. Many of my clients describe having their first panic attack during times of high stress. One client, who worked in sales, experienced his first attack after landing a high-profile client, even though he was excited about the prospect of managing the account. Another client had her first attack when she started medical school. Many clients report panic attacks in the midst of, or right after, an emotional breakup. Someone else started experiencing regular panic attacks when she left home for boarding school.

Chronic activation of the stress response takes a toll on your body. Problems such as muscle tension and headaches are often a direct response to stress, and a host of other illnesses are exacerbated by chronic stress. The good news is that many of the negative stress-related symptoms can be resolved with changes in how we care for ourselves, and by developing skills to combat the exaggerated stress responses of panic. One of those skills is acceptance, which we'll practice in the next exercise. Acceptance guides us to stop struggling against panic so that we move through it more quickly, and with less friction.

Acceptance of Unpleasant Physical Sensations

1. Pick a physical sensation that is difficult for you. You could start with a simple ache or pain that you typically ignore, such as a tight jaw. If you feel up for it, you could pick one of the physical sensations you experience during panic, like dizziness, breathlessness, or an increased heart rate.

2. Say aloud (or think) "I am willing to feel _____."

3. If you are working with a chronic ache or pain, simply turn your attention to that part of your body.

4. If you are working with a panic sensation, do an activity to induce the sensation. For instance, you could spin around to induce dizziness, breathe through a straw to induce breathlessness, or run up a flight of stairs to increase your heart rate.

5. Approach the sensation with a sense of open curiosity.

6. What do you notice? Label any thoughts that come up (e.g., "I am thinking I can't stand this").

7. When you are done, reflect on the experience. Were you really willing to experience the sensation? What would make you more willing? Did you notice anything new about the sensation? Did you notice a pattern to your thoughts? Did you engage in any subtle forms of distraction?

8. Take a deep breath, and as you exhale, let the experience go.

As mentioned earlier, taking slow, deep breaths communicates to your parasympathetic nervous system that everything is okay, and this can help you calm down. The next exercise is a good one to add to your regular routine.

Anchor in the Storm (Slow Breathing)

The point of this exercise is to slow your breathing as much as possible. Think of this breath pattern as your anchor in the emotional storm of panic. Practice it often when you are calm so it will come to you more easily in the midst of panic. If you can add to the counts described here, in order to slow down your breathing even more, do so.

1. Inhale slowly as you count to 5 (1-2-3-4-5).
2. Hold for 1 to 3 counts.
3. Exhale slowly as you count down from 5 (5-4-3-2-1).
4. Repeat.

Alternatively, you can trace a square with your finger (either in the air or on a table-top). As you draw the first side of the square, inhale; on the next side, hold; on the next, exhale, etc. Repeat the pattern of inhale-hold-exhale, matching each action to a side of your square.

Where Does Your Panic Show Up?

Now that we have covered what is happening in your body when you panic, let's take some time to think about specifically *where* those symptoms show up for *you*. If you close your eyes and think about your experiences with panic, is there a part of your body that immediately tenses up, like your shoulders? Because the panic experience can be so intense and all-consuming, and can come on unexpectedly at times, it may be difficult for you to recognize all the physiological sensations you experience. For some people, one panic sensation—hyperventilating, or feeling dizzy and faint, for example—is so dominant that it distracts you from others. The exact sensations you feel may vary from one panic attack to another, but because of the cycle of fear, most people have one or two aspects of the panic experience that are particularly scary for them. If this is the case for you, you may experience "tunnel vision" related to this sensation, meaning that when it occurs, your attention narrows in on that particular feeling and you pay less attention to everything else.

Other people describe having a "red-flag" sensation, like sweating or shaking, which signals to them that a full panic attack is about to come. This might be the physiological sensation they try to avoid the most, in an effort to reduce the likelihood of triggering a full-fledged panic attack. I once worked with a middle-aged man named Stephan who came to associate sweating and heat sensations with an impending panic attack. This led him to avoid a host of situations, from exercise to saunas to buildings without air conditioning. For some folks, panic feels so overwhelming and all-consuming that they simply describe the experience as losing control of their bodies, and they are less able to describe the distinct physiological sensations they experience. As we will explore later in this chapter, the more general body awareness you develop, the more you will be attuned to nuances in your physiology, which will eventually help you feel more comfortable with your physical experiences.

The next exercise will help you think carefully about your physical experiences during a panic attack.

Assessment of Physiological Symptoms

During a panic attack, which of the following physiological symptoms do you experience?

- ❑ Palpitations, pounding heart, or accelerated heart rate
- ❑ Sweating
- ❑ Trembling or shaking
- ❑ Sensations of shortness of breath or smothering
- ❑ Feelings of choking
- ❑ Chest pain or discomfort
- ❑ Nausea or other abdominal distress
- ❑ Dizziness
- ❑ Feeling unsteady, lightheaded, or faint
- ❑ Chills
- ❑ Heat sensations
- ❑ Numbness
- ❑ Tingling sensations
- ❑ Other: _____

_____

_____

Which of these sensations do you find the most uncomfortable or distressing?

_____

_____

_____

Having a clear understanding of where and how you most often experience the sensations of a panic attack is an important first step in helping you learn how to manage the symptoms and help yourself through them. Your body and your mind are intimately connected.

The Body-Mind Connection

Although you can't necessarily plan for or reliably prevent all panic attacks, there are many things you can do to reduce the likelihood that you'll have one, or increase the likelihood that you'll bounce back faster if panic does strike. If your body is under-rested, poorly nourished, or otherwise unhealthy, you are more vulnerable to anxiety and panic. Taking care of yourself physically is a great way to lay the foundation of your anti-panic program.

The aftermath of a panic attack is both mental and physical. In addition to feeling discouraged and scared, you will likely feel physically drained. As we discussed, because the fight-or-flight response involves the activation of many different bodily functions, in the wake of a panic attack you will probably feel wiped out. This is a critical time to take good care of yourself. Take a nap or find other ways to rest or relax in order to help your body recuperate. Anything you do to calm your residual anxiety will also encourage your body to stop releasing stress hormones, thus reducing their impact on your immune system. It will also be important to hydrate and to eat nutrient and protein rich foods to help you regain your strength and stamina. Taking care of yourself extends beyond the aftermath, of course. There are three important areas to focus on: sleep, nutrition, and exercise.

Sleep

Adequate sleep is fundamental to both physical and mental well-being. While we sleep, our bodies and brains regenerate themselves. Particularly during slow-wave sleep, our tissues and cells repair themselves, and brain chemical and hormone levels are balanced out. In fact, when laboratory rats are deprived of slow-wave sleep for several days, their brains begin to malfunction and they become physically sick.

People react to sleep deprivation in much the same way. If you think back to the last time you had a few nights of poor sleep, you'll likely remember feeling confused, achy, and emotional. If you're sleep deprived, you are much more likely to overreact and misinterpret benign physiological sensations as signs of impending danger, thus making panic attacks more likely. Similarly, if you experience a panic attack and have not had enough sleep, you'll likely be less able to cope well. Your brain won't be as quick to remind you of the strategies you've learned to calm yourself down, like slow breathing or engaging in calming self-talk.

The general rule of thumb is that eight hours of sleep per night is needed for optimal well-being (or seven to nine hours on average). If you consistently get less sleep than this, take a look at the following list of strategies that have been shown to improve your sleep, and circle the ones you're willing to try. Then put a check mark by three you'll start this week.

- ❏ Use your bed only for sleep (or sex) (e.g., no reading, streaming videos, or surfing the Internet).
- ❏ If you have been lying awake for more than 15 minutes, get out of bed until you feel drowsy.
- ❏ Don't get in bed until you feel drowsy.
- ❏ Avoid doing any stimulating activities before bed, including work or exercise.
- ❏ Wake up at (roughly) the same time each day and go to sleep at the same time each night.
- ❏ Avoid taking naps.
- ❏ Avoid drinking caffeine, especially after noon.
- ❏ Avoid alcohol late at night.
- ❏ Avoid bright light at night.
- ❏ Lower the temperature when you go to bed.
- ❏ If you start to worry or have negative thoughts when you get in bed, try to distract yourself or engage in a relaxation exercise, such as meditation.

Some people experience nocturnal panic attacks that cause them to wake up from sleep in a state of panic. These forms of panic can be particularly scary and disorienting, because they truly feel like they come out of nowhere, but you can handle them in the same way as ordinary panic attacks. Remind yourself that your body is having a normal reaction to fear that's happening at the wrong time. (In other words, remind yourself that you are having a panic attack and it will be over soon.) Engage in the slow breathing technique we talked about. Distract your senses by getting up and drinking a glass of cold water or a cup of warm tea. Listen to calming music or engage in a relaxation exercise. Try not to dwell on the experience, and get back to sleep as soon as you can.

Nutrition

Well-balanced nutrition is also essential to optimal physical and mental well-being. More and more research shows that a healthy diet is critical to managing anxiety and other mental health conditions. If you tend to eat a lot of processed foods and sugar, you are likely consuming a lot of simple carbohydrates, which can lead to drops in your blood sugar and increased experiences of feeling "jittery" or "on edge." In contrast, complex carbohydrates, found in beans, whole grains, and vegetables, help you maintain a more even blood sugar level, which is associated with feeling calm. It is also important to eat regularly. Skipping a meal could worsen your anxiety symptoms by leading to a drop in blood sugar.

Poor gut health has also been linked to higher rates of anxiety and depression. The two main food groups that can help you maintain good gut health are fiber and probiotics. Fiber-rich foods include raspberries, popcorn, artichokes, chickpeas, lentils, chia seeds, and oats. To increase your intake of probiotics, take probiotic supplements or eat probiotic-rich foods, like yogurt, kefir, pickles, and sauerkraut.

Other nutrients that have been linked to lower levels of anxiety include magnesium, zinc, omega-3 fatty acids, B vitamins, and antioxidants. One research study found that when mice were fed diets low in magnesium they exhibited increased anxiety-related behaviors. Magnesium-rich foods include leafy greens like spinach, as well as avocados, almonds, and dark chocolate. Even better, some of the magnesium-rich foods contain other anxiety-fighting properties. For instance, avocados and almonds are also rich in B vitamins, and spinach is also a good source of antioxidants. Zinc is found in cashews, liver, oysters, beef, and egg yolks. Eating salmon or sardines will increase your intake of omega-3 fatty acids.

Antioxidants are associated with a host of health benefits, including reduced anxiety. They are found in many fruits, like apples and blueberries, as well as in spices such as turmeric and ginger. If you don't like the specific foods mentioned here, you can always increase your intake of these nutrients with supplements (taken as directed, of course).

Putting all this nutrition information together, here is a sample anxiety-fighting menu:

Breakfast

Eggs and whole wheat toast

or

Yogurt with blueberries, raspberries, and chia seeds

Lunch

Sandwich on whole wheat bread with a pickle

or

Chicken with brown rice or salad

Snacks

Apple

Hummus with sliced veggies

Nuts (e.g., almonds, cashews, or walnuts)

Dinner

Salmon with spinach or broccoli

or

Taco salad with beef or black beans and guacamole

Some people find nutrition information a bit overwhelming, but when in doubt, just try to eat whole, unprocessed foods. Eating a diet rich in fruits, vegetables, and naturally occurring proteins, and avoiding junk food like potato chips, pizza, and ice cream, will help your body remain in balance and will give you a strong foundation to help you manage your anxiety.

Exercise

Like many people who experience panic, you may have a complicated relationship with exercise. The benefits of exercise include releasing "feel-good" hormones—like endorphins—calming your nervous system, and lowering your resting heart rate, all of which are associated with reduced levels of anxiety. Exercise can also boost your confidence. But as you probably know all too well, exercise also produces sensations that are almost identical to the symptoms you experience during a panic attack, including a racing pulse, breathlessness, and sweating. Because exertion activates your sympathetic nervous system, during a workout your body releases stress hormones like cortisol. People who experience panic are not only hyper-attuned to sympathetic nervous system arousal and increases in stress hormones, but are also more likely to interpret these experiences as dangerous, which only leads to more nervous system arousal and stress hormones. This is why exercise often triggers a full-fledged panic attack.

But the benefits of regular exercise are far too great to give up on it, even if you associate many of the sensations with panic. Some research has even found that regular exercise is as effective as anti-anxiety medications like selective serotonin reuptake inhibitors (SSRIs). In the short run, when you exercise you release endorphins, which are associated with feelings of euphoria and calm and increase your levels of the calming neurotransmitter gamma-aminobutyric acid, or GABA. In the long-term, exercise is associated with lower cortisol levels and decreased sympathetic nervous system reactivity.

Importantly for people who experience panic attacks, regular exercise can also help you become more comfortable with the physical sensations of panic. In other words, you will learn to tolerate sweating, an increased heart rate, and breathlessness, which will help you become more comfortable with the panic experience. Of course, for many people, this is easier said than done. The minute your heart rate increases, you may become immediately fearful that you are having an attack or that you might faint, which in turn further amps up your mental and physical fear response. If this is the case for you, try starting with less aerobic forms of exercise, such as weight lifting or walking. You can gradually build up to more intense and aerobic forms of exercise. Most importantly, just move your body regularly.

TARGETING BODILY SYMPTOMS: AMIR'S STORY

Amir always loved to run. As a young boy, he never slowed down. His mother used to say that he was "faster than the wind." As a high school freshman, Amir was already the star of the school's track team. He could run a mile in four minutes flat. After Amir's father lost his job, the burden of the household finances fell on him. Juggling school, track, and his job at the local grocery store started to take a toll on him. He stayed up very late each night trying to get his schoolwork done and worked extra shifts at the grocery store on the weekends.

One day on the track field, breathless from running, he started to hyperventilate. His mouth became dry and he quickly felt like he was choking. He yelled for help and was taken to the school nurse. By the time he got there, he was also trembling and experiencing blurred vision. His vital signs were all within normal limits, and eventually he calmed down. But the next time he went for a run, he started to feel like he was choking again. Scared to go through the same experience twice he slowed down to a jog. Eventually, even a light jog brought on the same sensations and he stopped running altogether.

It wasn't until he attended college and happened upon the track team practicing that he realized how much he missed running. He got checked out by a doctor and was assured he was in great physical health and could run without concern. Only then did Amir realize that what he had experienced was anxiety. Slowly, but surely, he began to take slow jogs around campus. He would still get dry mouth, but as long as he had enough water with him he could keep going. After a while he tried out for the track team. Not surprisingly, he made the team and soon he was back to winning most of the races he competed in.

Everyday Body Awareness

When we talked about mindfulness earlier in the book, we learned about the importance of maintaining awareness of and a sense of openness to our current experience. Panic attacks are mostly made up of short-lived physiological sensations that, though unpleasant, are ultimately not harmful. This means that learning to be more aware of your body and being open to experiencing a range of everyday physical sensations is a good place to start increasing your level of comfort with the panic experience. When you purposefully attune to your sensory experiences, you develop a sense of familiarity with your body that will ultimately help you feel more comfortable in your own skin, even when panic strikes.

This process begins by building awareness of your bodily sensations for *what they are* and placing less emphasis on *how you interpret them*. For instance, if you experience the sensations of tingling and numbness in your foot, your immediate interpretation might be, "My foot is asleep." To develop body awareness, you would place less emphasis on your automatic interpretation and focus more on the sensory experience—the tingling, coldness, numbness, and so on.

Developing more awareness of your body begins with mindfully engaging with your sensations in everyday activities like eating, washing dishes, or taking a shower. Before you take a bite of food, notice your hunger cues. Are you starving or mildly hungry? Do you notice any physical sensations, like slight salivation? When you swallow your food, notice the sensations in your mouth and throat. Notice your stomach. Can you feel the food reach your stomach? What hunger sensations are you experiencing now? Does your stomach still feel empty, or is it beginning to fill? When you wash dishes or take a shower, notice the sensations of the water touching your skin. Notice any temperature changes you experience. The more you engage with your sensations in this way, the more nuanced and less reactive your experience will become.

In addition to this mindful attention to your daily activities, you can also take a more focused, intentional approach to developing body awareness. For most people, this exercise has an added benefit of being very relaxing. Although you can do this exercise yourself, reading the instructions as you go and pausing at each step, you may wish to have someone read this aloud to you. You could even record yourself reading it so you can play it any time you wish.

Body Scan Meditation

Instructions: The following exercise can be done sitting in a chair or lying down on a firm surface. If sitting, maintain an upright posture with your feet firmly on the ground. Close your eyes, if that is comfortable for you.

Begin by taking a few deep breaths and trying to bring your awareness to your body.

As you inhale, envision bringing oxygen to every part of your body from the center of your being out to your extremities.

As you exhale, envision relaxing more fully and deeply with each breath.

As we go through the scan of your body from your toes moving upward, notice any tension you are holding. When you notice tension, exaggerate slightly by tensing the muscles more strongly and then releasing them, allowing yourself to relax fully.

Start your body scan by noticing your feet. If you are sitting, observe the sensation of your feet touching the floor. Notice the weight and pressure of your feet on the ground. If you are not sitting, notice whatever sensation or vibrations you may feel in your feet.

Now shift your attention to your legs. Notice the weight of your legs on the floor or against the chair. Notice any pressure or pulsing, any heaviness or lightness.

Bring your attention to your back. Notice the pressure of your back against the floor or chair.

Now bring your attention to your stomach. You can place your hand on your stomach while you take a deep breath in. Is your stomach tense or tight? Let it soften as you exhale and release any tension.

Notice your hands. See if you can allow your fingers to uncurl and soften.

Next, move your attention to your arms. Feel any sensations in your arms and then release as fully as you can.

Notice your shoulders. Are they lifted toward your ears? Let them be soft and relaxed.

Bring your attention to your neck. Move your neck gently to release any tension.

Notice your jaw and your facial muscles. Are you clenching your jaw? Is your tongue touching the roof of your mouth? Wiggle your face muscles to release.

Take a deep breath and shift your awareness to take in your entire body. As you inhale, envision bringing oxygen to every part of your body from the center of your being out to your extremities. As you exhale, envision relaxing more fully and deeply with each breath.

When you are ready, blink your eyes softly open.

This exercise is a good one to add to your regular practice. Because panic manifests so strongly in the body, taking good care of yourself—getting enough sleep, eating well, and moving your body—and developing and refining your body awareness will be important resources for you.

Key Takeaways

In this chapter we talked about your body and the physical signs of panic. Specifically, we covered:

- The physical sensations that typically comprise a panic attack, like dizziness and increased heart rate.

- The fact that a panic experience is your body's normal response to fear, but it's happening at the wrong time.

- The importance of maintaining good foundational health through rest, diet, and exercise in order to reduce and manage the panic experience.

- The importance of increasing our awareness of, and willingness to experience, bodily sensations, which will ultimately help us become more comfortable with the physical sensations of panic.

CHAPTER FOUR:

Your Brain and Panicky Thoughts

Because our thoughts directly influence our emotions, errors in the way we think can cause us unnecessary emotional pain. In particular, the physical sensation of panic is often exacerbated by the kind of faulty thinking we're all prone to at times. If we buy into our erroneous thinking, we actually prolong the panic—and nobody wants that. If you feel lightheaded and think it's a sign that you're having a stroke, for example, you will likely feel afraid, which in turn amplifies your body's fear reaction. It's a vicious cycle that prolongs your panic symptoms.

Correcting thinking errors can be tricky, because they're difficult to even notice—at least at first. This is why cognitive behavioral therapy calls our immediate, reactive thinking *automatic thoughts*. They happen so quickly we barely notice them, and instead we often focus on the emotion that is tied to the thought. Thoughts arise and then pass (if we let them), and our interpretations of those thoughts are colored by emotions and faulty thinking. This chapter will help you learn to approach your own thoughts a bit more objectively, so you can more easily spot your thinking errors and correct them before they get carried away.

What Your Thoughts Tell You About Panic

If you are struggling with panic, your thoughts probably tell you all sorts of inaccurate things about what panic attacks are and what you should do in response to them (e.g., "avoid closed-in places or activities that raise your heart rate"). Your thoughts may even be telling you that a panic attack can kill you.

I worked with a young woman named Sofia who was convinced that the choking sensations and difficulty breathing she experienced during panic could lead to suffocation and ultimately death. Because of this fear, she experienced increasingly intense panic sensations. Sofia described feeling as though she was being "choked by the air," or as if there were literally an invisible person choking her.

Understandably, this led her to make extreme changes in her life in order to avoid panic. She barely left the house, and even moved into a new apartment to be closer to emergency care. Eventually, with professional support, she became willing to exert herself if she was right outside an urgent care setting. When panic was triggered, as her therapist I would stand next to her, repeating this statement out loud: "This is a panic attack. It cannot kill you." Eventually, she was able to say it to herself, and in turn her panic sensations became less and less extreme, providing her with further proof that her panic symptoms wouldn't kill her.

The more aware you can be about what your panic thoughts are telling you, the more consciously you can weigh the evidence for them. Start by being open to other explanations: Is it possible that the pain in your chest is due to a sore muscle, rather than a sign that you are having a heart attack? By asking yourself these types of questions, you bring the more logical side of your brain back into the conversation and lessen your fear reactions. Even if a part of you still thinks it might be a heart attack, being open to alternative explanations is the first step in shifting your thought patterns. In turn this will help you avoid making dramatic behavior changes for the wrong reasons.

This exercise will help you practice coming up with alternative explanations for the typical sensations you may experience during a panic attack. If you can come up with more than one possible interpretation, go for it!

What Are Your Thoughts Telling You?

Next to each physiological sensation listed below, write your typical first thought in response to that sensation. In the next column, write the other (likely more realistic) possible explanation(s) for each sensation. When you are not panicking, some of your immediate thoughts may be obviously false to you, but if they happen when you are in the midst of panic, write them down anyway. If you do not typically experience one of the sensations listed, either skip it or write down an interpretation you think you might have if it were to occur.

Physiological Sensation	Immediate Thought	Other Possible Interpretation
Chest pain or discomfort	"I am having a heart attack."	Indigestion or a sign of tension/stress
Palpitations, pounding heart, or accelerated heart rate		
Sweating		
Trembling or shaking		
Sensations of shortness of breath or smothering		
Feelings of choking		
Chest pain or discomfort		
Nausea or other abdominal distress		

Physiological Sensation	Immediate Thought	Other Possible Interpretation
Dizziness		
Feeling unsteady, lightheaded, or faint		
Chills or heat sensations		
Other:		

Revisit this exercise now and then, and over time perhaps you'll notice slight shifts in your automatic thoughts. You may be able to add to your list of other possible interpretations, too.

Examining the way you think about panic goes beyond thinking about specific symptoms. Panic is maintained by the way we think about it, and like anything else, it's possible to have mistaken beliefs that we may not even question. The next exercise explores 15 common beliefs about panic.

Beliefs About Panic

Response options:

4 = completely agree

3 = agree somewhat

2 = neither agree nor disagree

1 = disagree somewhat

0 = completely disagree

Instructions: Using the 5-point scale, indicate your level of agreement with the various beliefs people have about panic. Base your answers on what you've come to believe or what you believe in the midst of panic, as opposed to what you think you should believe.

1. I can't deal with panicky feelings alone. _____

2. I need to be able to access help at all times. _____

3. I won't be able to function if I have a panic attack. _____

4. If I start to panic, I need to escape the situation immediately. _____

5. A panic attack can kill me. _____

6. A panic attack can give me a heart attack. _____

7. A panic attack can cause lasting physical damage. _____

8. It is dangerous to carry on with my usual activities during a panic attack. _____

9. There is only so much anxiety my body can take. _____

10. Panicking while driving could lead me to crash. _____

11. A panic attack could cause me to lose control of my body. _____

12. A panic attack could cause me to lose control of my mind. _____

13. There is something physically wrong with me that the doctors just haven't found yet. _____

14. If people see me having a panic attack they will lose respect for me. _____

15. I must be on guard or I could miss a fatal physical symptom. _____

Total Score: _____

Interpretation:

15 or under: No faulty beliefs about panic

15 to 30: Low to mild faulty beliefs about panic

30 to 45: Faulty/distorted beliefs about panic

46+: Highly skewed/distorted beliefs about panic

Were you surprised by your score? You may wish to return to this exercise in the future to track changes in your beliefs. Remember that it's always important to rate each item based on what you *actually* believe rather than what you think you should believe. Understanding your own true beliefs, especially the distorted ones, is key to achieving the changes you want to make.

Common Thinking Errors

The first step to unraveling your distorted thought patterns is to catch yourself in the act. That way you can learn to address the thoughts as they arise, so they begin to have less influence on your emotions and behaviors. Learning about the different forms of common thinking errors can help you do this. As I mentioned earlier, most people immediately recognize at least one category of error in their own thinking. See if you recognize your own thoughts in any of the examples described here.

Catastrophizing is one of the most common thinking errors for people who experience panic. When you catastrophize, you focus on the worst possible outcome. You may think that the tight sensation in your chest means you're having a heart attack or is a sign of cancer. Maybe you assume you will get fired after making a small mistake at work. You may avoid an elevator because you think the elevator will break, you will become stuck, and you'll panic and make a fool of yourself. To work on your tendency to catastrophize, you might ask yourself to list other possible outcomes: What is the best possible outcome? What is a more realistic possible outcome?

Jumping to conclusions or predicting the future is another cognitive tendency that is common with anxiety. With this thought pattern, you always expect the worst. You assume that you will have a panic attack at an important work event or that your anxiety will ruin your vacation. This faulty assumption may even cause you to miss your work event or cancel your vacation. Working with acceptance can be helpful. If you were to accept that you may have some anxiety while on vacation, but also recognize that you don't have to let it ruin your vacation, you would more likely go ahead and have a relaxing trip. When you catch yourself predicting the future, start by reminding yourself that you really don't know what will happen. You might have a panic attack, but it is also possible that you won't have a panic attack.

Tunnel vision is another thinking error that is associated with anxiety, and one that is particularly common during panic sensations. This occurs when you focus intensely on threat-related information and pay no attention to signs of safety. For instance, someone engaging in tunnel vision would be focused on the information they found on the Internet, which suggested that dizziness may be a sign of a stroke, while not considering the fact that they recently underwent a full medical examination and that they stood up quickly right before they felt dizzy. When you catch yourself engaging in tunnel vision, encourage yourself to search for possible signs of safety or evidence that you are okay.

Emotional reasoning occurs when you take your emotions as *de facto* logic, such as assuming that because you feel anxious, something bad is going to occur. The more anxious you feel, the more certain you are of impending problems. Emotional reasoning is not always negative; the term *rose-colored glasses* refers to emotional reasoning that's working in a positive direction. Because you are happy, you're quick to notice all the nice things and kind people around. Negative emotional reasoning is the same process, just going in the other direction. When we are in a bad mood or feeling hopeless, we are more likely to remember all the times things went wrong. When you catch yourself engaging in negative emotional reasoning, try to specifically think back to a time when things went right or worked out better than you expected.

Overgeneralization occurs when you take a single example or instance of something and assume it will continue to happen. For example, if you are rejected when you ask someone out on a date, you assume that no one will ever want to go out with you. Or if you have a panic attack when you are out on a date, you assume it will always happen and that you shouldn't go out again. When you catch yourself overgeneralizing (key words to attend to are *always* and *never*), force yourself to think about the other possibilities. Remind yourself that just because something happened once does not mean that it will always happen that way.

If you're still having difficulty catching your own thinking errors, you can start by working backward and begin with the distressing emotion. When you have a distressing emotion, try to slow down and capture what you said to yourself right before you got upset. Ask yourself what it was about the situation that upset you so much. What were you thinking right before your panic amped up? It can also help to write your thoughts down as quotes, as close to verbatim as possible, so you can analyze your specific, actual thinking to detect any distortions. Once you know you are engaging in a thinking error, you can begin to develop a more balanced viewpoint by asking yourself a series of questions to ponder alternative possible scenarios and by testing your assumptions in reality.

The next exercise allows you to explore your own thinking errors.

Identifying Your Thinking Errors

Use this form to write down thinking errors that are typical for you. Identifying these thoughts ahead of time will also help you learn to catch yourself in the act.

Type of Thinking Error	Examples That Are Typical for You
Catastrophizing	
Jumping to conclusions or predicting the future	
Tunnel vision	
Emotional reasoning	
Overgeneralization	

As you begin to work on understanding your panic experiences, it can be very helpful to keep a log so you can track important issues like physical symptoms and pre-attack thoughts. Thinking of your last panic attack, complete the log entry on the next page. If you like, you can maintain a journal where you log all these details over the coming months.

Panic Log

Date:_____ Time started:_____ Time ended:_____

Situation: _____

Did you expect this panic attack? Yes / No

What symptoms did you experience? Circle the symptoms that were the most distressing to you.

- ❑ Palpitations, pounding heart, or accelerated heart rate
- ❑ Sweating
- ❑ Trembling or shaking
- ❑ Sensations of shortness of breath or smothering
- ❑ Feelings of choking
- ❑ Chest pain or discomfort
- ❑ Nausea or abdominal distress
- ❑ Feeling dizzy, unsteady, lightheaded, or faint
- ❑ Chills or heat sensations
- ❑ Paresthesia (numbness or tingling sensations)
- ❑ Derealization (feelings of unreality)
- ❑ Depersonalization (feeling detached from yourself)
- ❑ Fear of losing control or "going crazy"
- ❑ Fear of dying
- ❑ Other: _____

Think about the period before the attack began. What were you thinking and doing?

Thoughts: _____

_____

Behaviors:_____

_____

What was your level of discomfort-on a scale of 1 to 10, 1 (minimal) to 10 (extreme)? _____

    Keeping notes about your experiences and learning to understand and detect your thinking errors can provide useful information. Now that you've identified your thinking errors and come up with a few alternative possibilities, it's time to put them to the test.

Testing Your Theories

Developing more realistic thoughts and beliefs begins with being willing to consider all the evidence. Hypothesis testing is one of the techniques used in cognitive behavioral therapy to help you change the way you think about certain events, emotions, and sensations, especially when your thinking is causing you problems or making your anxiety worse. Because it isn't always easy to just change the way we think, hypothesis testing is a tool you can use to actually begin to believe what you are trying to convince yourself about. The hypothesis is your belief or theory, and if you are willing to "test it" in the same way that a scientist would test an initial theory, or a detective would think through a possible explanation, you may come to recognize that your belief is actually unfounded.

If you believe that having a panic attack in public would cause anyone who saw it to lose respect for you, for example, or that it would cause your loved ones to cut you out of their lives, a way to test this theory would be to let someone see you have a panic attack. You may be surprised to learn that instead of rejecting you, the person offers you comfort and reassurance. They might even share with you some of their own anxieties or insecurities.

Of course, true hypothesis testing usually takes more than one round. For instance, in this scenario, your first test experience may simply allow you to modify your belief. You might think, "Well, I guess not *everyone* would reject me," and then quickly rationalize your initial theory by telling yourself, "But she happens to be a particularly kind and understanding person. Most people would still reject me or at least lose some respect for me." You would probably have to let a few more people see you panic before you were convinced that having anxiety and panic symptoms would not change the way people think about you.

If you were a scientist or detective, you wouldn't just settle on the first explanation you came to. You would likely spend time brainstorming and trying to think through *every* possible scenario you could think of. Then you would take each possible scenario and weigh the evidence for or against it. After coming to the most likely explanation, you would likely run further tests to make sure it held up. Take the same approach with your own beliefs and assumptions. Be as objective as possible in weighing the evidence for or against your beliefs as you try to come to the most logical and likely explanation.

Testing Your Theories

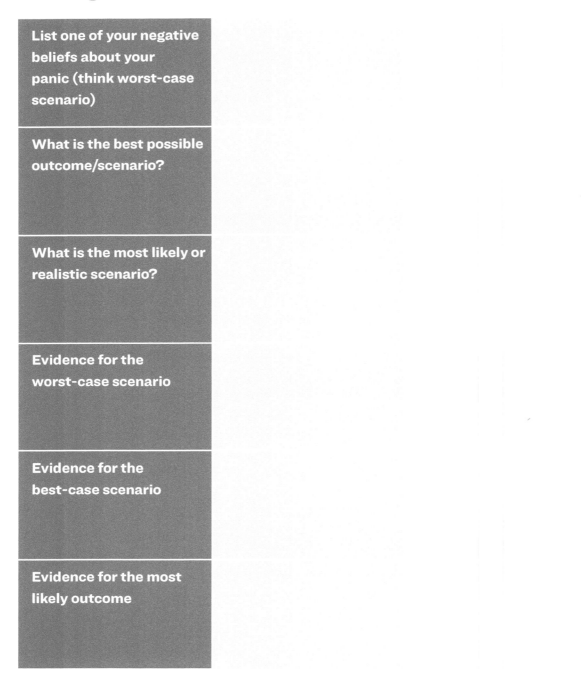

List one of your negative beliefs about your panic (think worst-case scenario)

What is the best possible outcome/scenario?

What is the most likely or realistic scenario?

Evidence for the worst-case scenario

Evidence for the best-case scenario

Evidence for the most likely outcome

This exercise of considering the evidence for a number of scenarios is a very useful beginning, and then you'll want to take your theories out for a spin.

Testing Your Theories in Real Life

Pick a belief or hypothesis to test in real life, following the approach described on page 57 in the example of having a panic attack in public. After testing it out, use the following questions to reflect upon what you learned in your first round of hypothesis testing.

What belief/hypothesis did you test?

_____

_____

_____

What was your worst fear related to this belief?

_____

_____

_____

How accurate was your belief?

_____

_____

_____

What did you learn from this experience?

_____

_____

_____

How has this new information modified your prior belief/hypothesis?

_____

_____

_____

Just as in the earlier example, you may find yourself thinking of some way to rationalize the experience so you can hang on to your belief. If this happens, test it again, as many times as it takes to recognize a shift in your belief.

TARGETING COGNITIVE SYMPTOMS: GABRIELA'S STORY

Gabriela watched her grandfather die slowly from cancer when she was six years old. Since then, she developed intense fears surrounding illness and death. At the first sign of chicken pox, she ran to find her mother, sobbing, worried she was dying. When she got a bad flu as a teenager, she was sure she had contracted malaria. Shortly after having her first child, Gabriela experienced what she thought was a heart attack. She and her baby were alone at the time, so she called an ambulance to get to the hospital.

After undergoing an electrocardiogram (EKG) recording, she was informed that there were no major electrical changes detected in her heart and that she had likely experienced a panic attack. Despite experiencing recent increases in her overall levels of anxiety and worry related to having a baby, Gabriela was not convinced. The experience had been so scary, she was sure the doctors were missing something. Maybe she'd had a stroke that was harder to detect?

A few weeks later she experienced another episode of chest discomfort and difficulty breathing, and she became dizzy and lightheaded. Maybe it was a brain tumor? Again, after rushing to urgent care, Gabriela was assured that none of the tests indicated that anything was physically wrong with her, and the doctors again suggested that she was likely experiencing panic attacks. Gabriela did her own research and had to admit that all her symptoms were described as symptoms of panic. Still, she was convinced that something was wrong. There was no way her intense physiological sensations were "just anxiety." After each panic attack, Gabriela went to urgent care, where she was repeatedly assured that everything was fine. The frequent urgent care visits began to take a toll financially, and she found it difficult to maintain employment due to regular absences. The attacks also disrupted her social life and time spent with her family.

Eventually, she recognized that she was suffering from panic disorder. She stopped visiting urgent care, but kept up more than regular doctors' visits. Finally, with the help of her family, she recognized that the doctors' visits were a way she soothed herself post-panic and were not required for her health. Although she still expresses the urge to go to urgent care and make sure everything is okay, she is also enjoying getting her life back.

Learning to Reframe Your Thoughts

Reframing your thinking occurs when you discover, challenge, and then modify or replace your negative, irrational thoughts. In other words, you come up with a different interpretation of an event or experience. In doing so, you can change the way you feel about it. When you're able to develop more positive, or at least more realistic, ways of thinking, the result is usually reduced anxiety and a better mood. In the beginning, it can be helpful to write down your thoughts in order to objectively analyze them. With time, reframing your thoughts will become easier and more automatic.

So how does reframing work? Start by thinking about (or writing down) a given problem or situation. Let's say you are dreading an upcoming plane trip because you are worried you will have a panic attack while in flight and won't have anywhere to go. Let yourself think through all the things that concern you about that situation. You might be concerned that you won't be able to get up from your seat and will be seated tightly between two strangers while panicking. You might be worried that if your panic spirals out of control, there won't be a doctor or medical professional on board to make sure you are okay. At the very least, you think you will be horribly embarrassed.

How does this type of thinking make you feel? Most likely it leaves you feeling anxious and worried. Now think through some possible alternative scenarios. Even if you don't think they are likely, come up with at least four possible options.

- Maybe you won't have a panic attack.

- Maybe you will have a panic attack, but no one will seem to notice.

- Maybe you will have a panic attack, but it will be during a point in the flight when you can get up, excuse yourself, and splash cold water on your face.

- Maybe you will have a noticeable panic attack, people will look at you, and then you will get off the plane and go on your way.

Now consider any evidence to support these alternative possibilities. For instance, maybe you took a flight recently and didn't have a panic attack. Or maybe you did panic, but it wasn't as bad as you imagined it would be. As the ancient Roman philosopher Seneca once said, "We suffer more in imagination than in reality."

Reframing your thinking doesn't mean you have to make the jump all the way from negative thinking to positive thinking. You can start with trying to shift your negative thoughts to more neutral thoughts. You won't necessarily go from being convinced that you will have a panic attack and it will be awful to being convinced that you won't have a panic attack and everything will be great, but you might be able to shift to thinking that you may or may not have a panic attack or that it might not be so awful.

Reviewing your panic logs will help you identify thought patterns and begin the reframing process. When experiencing panic, you will likely jump quickly to engaging in catastrophic thinking and emotional reasoning. What if I am about to faint? This feels so awful, something bad must be about to happen. When you are calm, you can more easily see your tendencies to exaggerate or overreact, but in the moment, it can be harder to catch yourself. Review the alternative explanations for unwanted bodily sensations that you worked through in the "What Are Your Thoughts Telling You?" exercise (see page 49). Some people find it helpful to put their alternative interpretations on a flashcard or small piece of paper so they can carry it with them as a reminder when panic strikes. In the next chapter we will start the process of facing some of those situations and sensations you fear and avoid. This will help provide you with further evidence to use for reframing your thoughts.

For now, this exercise will give you practice reframing the kinds of thinking errors you tend to make.

Reframing Your Thinking Errors

Use the table below to help you identify and correct your typical thinking errors. If you aren't able to catch your irrational thoughts right away, just start with thoughts that cause you to feel upset and then determine if each thought is exaggerated or extreme.

Remember that the common thinking errors are:

- Catastrophizing

- Jumping to conclusions or predicting the future

- Tunnel vision

- Emotional reasoning

- Overgeneralization

Distressing thought	What type of thinking error is this?	Alternative explanations: What is a more balanced/realistic way of thinking about this?

Testing your beliefs and developing alternative explanations are great tools for working with distorted thinking. Another important aspect of these thinking errors relates to the probability of the scenarios happening. The next exercise will teach you how to determine that likelihood when working with your distorted thoughts.

Developing Realistic Odds

The goal of this exercise is to help you become more realistic in your thinking about panic. Start with one of your negative beliefs about panic sensations and then work through other possible explanations for that sensation.

List one of your negative beliefs about a panic sensation: _____
_____

Fill in the circles in this exercise like a pie chart, with the largest piece of the pie representing the most likely scenario.

The first circle represents your initial beliefs, or the beliefs you have during panic. So, if you are 100 percent sure that the discomfort in your chest during panic signals that you're having a heart attack, the circle will not be divided, and you will simply write "heart attack" in the middle. If you are 90 percent sure you are having a heart attack, but recognize that there is a 10 percent chance your chest pain is due to anxious thoughts, divide the pie accordingly. Now take the negative belief you listed earlier and divide the pie.

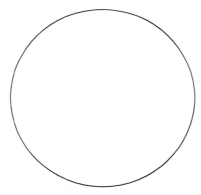

Next, think through all the possible alternative scenarios. What is the evidence for or against each of these possibilities? Complete the circle again, this time trying to be as realistic as possible and including your alternative scenarios.

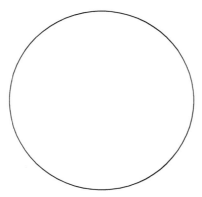

For many people, having a handy visual way of thinking about things is helpful. If this is you, explore other negative beliefs you have during panic.

Working with panic attacks is focused on managing the experience itself, but you also want to track your progress over time. Otherwise, it can be hard to get a good sense of what is changing, how and where you should direct your attention, and whether you have frequent attacks or occasional ones. You might learn a lot about your attacks by maintaining the panic log you completed earlier in this chapter (see page 55). It's also helpful to take a big-picture view of your progress.

Panic Attack Progress Record

Use the chart on page 67 to track the number of panic attacks you have each week. Each week, place a mark in the box that corresponds to the number of times you experienced panic during that week. This will not only help you track your progress, but can also help you detect patterns or factors that make your panic worse or better. If you notice that during a given week you had more panic attacks than is typical for you, think about why. Were you under more stress? Did you get less sleep? Were you less willing to try your breathing exercises? If you notice that during a given week you had fewer panic attacks than is typical, think about why. Did you implement a new coping strategy? Were you able to reframe your thinking more than usual?

Panic Attacks (#)	Week 1 Date: ____	Week 2 Date: ____	Week 3 Date: ____	Week 4 Date: ____	Week 5 Date: ____	Week 6 Date: ____	Week 7 Date: ____	Week 8 Date: ____
10								
9								
8								
7								
6								
5								
4								
3								
2								
1								
0								

Key Takeaways

In this chapter we explored thoughts and beliefs surrounding panic and learned how panic can be fueled by our thinking. Specifically, we covered:

- Common problematic thought patterns.

- Your specific thoughts and beliefs that may be contributing to your panic attacks.

- A number of tools to help you challenge any thinking errors you may be engaging in.

- Ways to break the link between your thoughts and unhelpful behaviors.

- How to critically examine the beliefs you hold about panic and its aftermath.

- New, more balanced ways of thinking about panic sensations.

CHAPTER FIVE:

Your Behavior and Fear-Based Avoidance

So far, we've talked about the signs of panic that you experience in your body and the types of thought patterns that often accompany these physical symptoms. In this chapter, we are going to target the panic-related behaviors that may be causing you problems: namely, avoidance and escape behaviors. You probably engage in these behaviors in order to *avoid* or *lessen* your panic and anxiety symptoms, and this strategy often works in the short run. Unfortunately, the more you avoid situations or physical sensations that you fear will cause you to panic, the more panic and anxiety you will experience over the long run. This is because avoiding anxiety-provoking situations and sensations tricks your brain into thinking that the false alarm it received was actually valid, thus strengthening the association your brain has with the situation and a fear response. In other words, anxiety causes avoidance behaviors, and avoidance behaviors cause more anxiety.

Another thing to remember is that the more you avoid things that cause you anxiety, the more your day-to-day life will be disrupted by your anxiety. If you avoid crowded places out of fear that you won't be able to get out quickly enough, you will be more likely to have panic attacks in crowds. Plus, in the long run, you will be more likely to miss out on enjoyable activities and important life events, like movies and concerts, or a family member's graduation ceremony.

In contrast, when you confront these scary situations, you provide yourself with opportunities to learn new things about how you'll respond in the situation, and you also give yourself the chance to learn that the situation is harmless or that you have the skills to cope with your anxiety and panic. This reduces your anxiety about the situation and weakens your brain's association between the situation and your fear reaction. Additionally, you'll be able to do more of the things in life that matter to you.

The Avoidance Trap

As humans evolved, we learned to avoid anything we perceived as dangerous. This is a helpful adaptive behavior because it protects us from harm and keeps us vigilant. The problem is that anxious minds often make up threats where there really are none. When we are in the grips of panic, we're likely to see these threats as catastrophic or life-threatening. If we let this anxious but inaccurate thinking guide our decisions about where it's safe to go and what it's safe to do, our lives will just get smaller and smaller and our anxiety will grow. The tricky thing about avoidance behavior is that it really seems to work. If you think you will have a panic attack in the grocery store and might pass out or throw up in front of lots of people, you will feel a huge sense of relief when someone like your roommate or family member offers to go for you. This pleasant feeling reinforces your avoidance behavior, so you become less and less likely to go to the store. It works for you in the moment, so you keep doing it.

Over time, however, you will actually *increase* your anxiety because you are reinforcing inaccurate beliefs about perceived danger and teaching yourself that avoidance works. The more caught up you get in the avoidance trap, the more you will notice your behavior change. For example, you might start out avoiding the grocery store during peak shopping hours, but after a while you start avoiding any grocery store that is far from your home. Or maybe you notice that you never go to the grocery store alone for fear of panicking without someone there to help you.

The pull of the avoidance trap can be so powerful that you might find yourself making major life changes because of your anxiety, like quitting a job you love to avoid using elevators or driving on freeways, or making major changes in your social life. I worked with a woman named Maria who experienced extreme nausea during panic and felt as though she might defecate. She became worried that she would defecate in her pants during a panic attack and thought she would metaphorically "die of embarrassment" if that happened. Maria eventually broke up with her boyfriend due to her fear that it would happen while she was out with him, thus losing a relationship that was actually very important to her.

You might also notice that you develop a strong attachment to objects that help you feel safe and calm, like a cell phone so you can call someone for help, or a water bottle to help you manage sensations of dry mouth or choking. Maybe you never leave home without fast-acting anxiety medications or a superstitious object, like an angel key chain or other lucky charm. Do you engage in excessive safety behaviors, like planning out an escape route every time you enter a new building or remaining in close proximity to exit locations when you are inside? The more excessive safety measures you engage in, the more distracted from your life you will become. If you are at a holiday party but repeatedly have to check that your exit route remains unobstructed, you might have difficulty maintaining a conversation with your friends or spouse, thus impacting your relationships and your ability to enjoy the party. If you leave the party or grocery store because of your fears that you might panic (that is, you escape the situation), your brain is telling you that your fear was justified.

Avoidance can sometimes be hard to catch. Many people use substances, food, or other forms of distraction like shopping to avoid feeling their emotions, including anxiety. This form of avoidance is less obvious than avoiding situations or activities that induce unpleasant sensations, but it can be equally impactful on your life and anxiety levels. To consider this type of avoidance behavior, ask yourself, "Is there anything I do in response to my anxiety that seems to help, but actually causes me problems over time?" Or maybe, "What tools do I use to numb my anxiety and fears about panic?"

Your avoidance behavior might primarily stem from avoidance of a particular situation, like panicking in public places, or it might be driven primarily by a desire to avoid an unpleasant physical sensation, like shortness of breath or the sensation of being light-headed. For many people it is a combination of both. It can be helpful to think about what is driving your avoidance behavior in order to help you develop a plan for confronting your fears, and to help you decide which coping strategies to use in the process.

The next exercise will take you through the issues raised so far in this chapter.

What Are You Avoiding?

Take a moment to think about some of your own avoidance behaviors. What are the things that you are NOT doing in order to avoid the possibility of another panic attack?

What *situations* do you avoid due to concerns about panic?

_____

_____

_____

What *activities* do you avoid due to concerns about inducing panic?

_____

_____

_____

What *things* do you do to avoid experiencing particular physical sensations?

_____

_____

_____

Are there *objects* that you use to manage your panic that you won't leave home without or that you always have with you?

_____

_____

_____

Do you engage in any excessive *safety behaviors* to manage your panic?

_____

_____

_____

With the details of what you do (or rather *don't* do) in hand, it's time to consider what you are getting from this coping approach.

Why Are You Avoiding It?

Now that you know *what* you are avoiding, let's take a minute to think about *why*. We only persist in doing things from which we receive a benefit, even though that benefit might be hidden underneath all the problems those things cause.

What beliefs do you have about panic that encourage you to avoid it?

_____

_____

_____

How do you feel right after you avoid a fear-ridden situation? (e.g., calm, safe, relieved)

_____

_____

_____

What are the good things about your avoidance behaviors? (e.g., "helps me feel safe")

_____

_____

_____

Your answers to those questions are probably pretty positive—you feel better, and the avoidance behaviors help you feel safe. So what's the problem?

The Cost of Avoidance

Avoidance usually comes at a cost. Use the questions here to explore what avoidance might be costing you.

How have you changed your life to avoid or manage panic?

_____

_____

_____

What are the downsides of these changes?

_____

_____

_____

Are there any activities you have stopped doing in order to avoid a panic attack?

_____

_____

_____

Have you missed out on any important life events because you were avoiding anxiety or panic? If so, what have you missed out on?

_____

_____

_____

Whether you see small losses for now, or you recognize significant changes to your life as a result of your avoidance behaviors, the good news is that you aren't stuck with this coping strategy.

Alternatives to Avoidance

An important first step in breaking the habit of avoidance is thinking about *why* we want to make a change, and identifying what we could do instead. The alternatives to avoidance include learning different ways to think about anxiety, adopting different ways to cope with it, and finding different ways to react to it.

Let's start with the *why*. Hopefully by now you are at least partially convinced that avoidance has the paradoxical effect of increasing anxiety in the long run. Additionally, anxiety-driven avoidance usually costs you more and more of your ability to live a rich, full, and values-driven life. Once you know what you are avoiding and why, you can develop alternatives to your avoidance strategies and to your escape and safety-seeking behaviors.

I worked with a young sales professional in his midthirties, whom I'll call Mateo. At Mateo's company, the top sales professionals each year were rewarded with a luxury vacation for themselves and a guest. Mateo was particularly looking forward to taking his wife on a vacation because things had been a little rocky in their marriage. However, Mateo was terrified that he would have a panic attack on the plane and would not be able to get help. Even if he didn't have a panic attack, he was worried that he would drink too much, which he often did when he thought panic was around the corner. Either way, he didn't want to embarrass himself in front of the company's top executives, or start a fight with his wife.

Mateo was ready to get some help for his anxiety so he could learn new ways of dealing with it. So he started with a willingness to try to react differently to his anxiety. After learning some basic mindfulness techniques, he tried them when he became anxious, as opposed to immediately reaching for a beer to calm himself down. When he started to feel anxious he worked on pausing, and then identifying and describing his experience of the anxiety (e.g., "my thoughts are telling me _____, I feel _____ in my body"). In session, Mateo talked about what he feared the most, which was having a panic attack while flying over the ocean, and we did some structured visualization exercises related to his fears. Eventually, he went on a simulated flight through a program offered for people who experience anxiety. Next, he went on a local flight and eventually took the flight overseas with his company executives and his wife.

He had a few panic attacks along the way, but because he had worked on changing his relationship to his panic symptoms, he no longer drank excessively in anticipation of panic and found that, although unpleasant, his attacks were relatively brief. He was able to enjoy himself on the trip and came back feeling more confident about managing his anxiety and panic.

Mateo's story shows us how cultivating an overall attitude of courage can be a powerful antidote to avoidance behaviors. As Brené Brown writes in her book *Daring Greatly*, "[t]he willingness to show up changes us, it makes us a little braver each time." She also says that if you are "brave with your life and choose to live in the arena . . . [y]ou are going to fall and fail." Developing and maintaining an attitude of courage and willingness includes a readiness to experience hard emotions, including embarrassment and shame. The benefit to this approach is that you will start to feel stronger and will live a richer, more authentic life.

If you recognize that you are being brave and making important changes by simply *trying* not to avoid what scares you, you will have already made a shift away from avoidance behaviors. Give yourself credit for simply showing up in the arena. Try to focus less on the outcome of changing your avoidance behaviors and more on your willingness to try new ways of being and responding to anxiety. Developing an attitude of courage is going to require you to think courageous thoughts (e.g., "I can do this even if it is hard") and to do hard things, like facing head-on the things that scare you. Recognize your courage every step of the way.

Identify Alternative Behaviors

Now that you have identified some of the situations and sensations that you avoid, think about other ways to do things. For this exercise, brainstorm as many alternative behaviors that you can think of.

Avoidance Urge	Alternative Behaviors	Difficulty Rating (100% = Most Difficult)
Example: Have roommate go to the grocery store for me	Go to store with my roommate	70%
	Go to small store alone during off hours	85%
	Go to store by myself during peak shopping hours	99%
Example: Don't do activities that make me feel short of breath so I don't panic	Run at full speed	100%
	Jog	90%
	Yoga	50%
	Walk	5%

Avoidance Urge	Alternative Behaviors	Difficulty Rating (100% = Most Difficult)

If you rated any of the alternative scenarios 90 percent or above, you may have felt anxious or scared even thinking about them. You are courageous and willing to try new approaches to your anxiety, so your next step is to figure out how to get started.

How Scary Are Your Alternative Behaviors?

Review the list of "alternative behaviors" that you came up with in the exercise on page 79. Transfer your responses here, ordering them in terms of how scary they are to you, as indicated in the scale on this page. Eventually, you will actually do the things on this list! Start with one of the scenarios that is the least scary to you. Alternatively, continue to learn more about exposure before getting started and use this list to help organize your exposure exercises later.

	Feared Alternative Behaviors
Scariest scenarios	
Still scary	
Less scary	
Only a little fear	
Doesn't scare me	

Developing alternatives to avoidance and doing what is scary to you is the essence of exposure therapy, which we will discuss more in the next section. You don't have to wait to learn more about exposure to get started. Just do some of those things you have been avoiding.

TARGETING AVOIDANCE BEHAVIOR: KELLY'S STORY

When she was a little girl, Kelly noticed that her mom didn't leave the house much and didn't have many friends, but she never understood why. Eventually, Kelly learned that her mother suffered from intense anxiety. Kelly was sure she didn't want her own life to be so lonely, so she made friends with almost everyone she met and found so much joy in the time she spent with other people.

As she got older and her career progressed, Kelly found it increasingly difficult to keep up with her demanding job and social calendar. One day, while rushing to complete a stressful work assignment so she could make it to a friend's birthday party, Kelly felt short of breath, faint, dizzy, and nauseated. She knew enough about anxiety to recognize that she was having a panic attack, and her immediate thought was, "*I am going to turn into my mother.*" The thought filled her with such dread that her panic sensations amplified. She thought she was going to faint and called for a colleague to assist her.

Her fiancé had always nagged her about overbooking herself, so he was happy to hear her recognize that she needed to reduce her stress and cut back on some social engagements. At first this did reduce her stress, and she did not have another panic attack for a few weeks. But every time she canceled a social engagement, Kelly confirmed her fears that she was becoming more and more like her mother, which also increased her fears of debilitating panic attacks that would "ruin her life." Soon, she was having panic attacks even when she was at home and felt calm. She also became increasingly embarrassed about missing social events she used to enjoy, and began to avoid more and more of her friends. Eventually, it got to the point where she missed her best friend's wedding, due to her fears that running into so many people she had canceled on would cause her to panic and make a scene at the event. Not only did she miss the wedding, but she had one of her worst panic attacks anyway. Kelly's fiancé, who had initially been supportive of her efforts to reduce her stress, was now concerned. He did not recognize her anymore.

Kelly was able to recognize that she had fallen into the same avoidance trap as her mother had, and the realization motivated her to make a change. She started by calling all the friends she had been avoiding and simply told them why. She was comforted and encouraged by their warm responses and understanding. She still did not feel up for a crowded social event, but agreed to meet a good friend for coffee. She had a panic attack on the way to the meeting, but went anyway, all the while reminding herself that she did not want to repeat her family patterns. This was the major turning point for Kelly, who continued to reduce her panic attacks and return to the life she loved.

Get Some Exposure

Decades of research show that exposure techniques are the most effective treatment for anxiety. By intentionally and systematically exposing yourself to the situations and sensations you fear, you retrain your brain to stop sending fear signals when there is no real danger. The portion of your brain that's responsible for fear, the amygdala, is fairly primitive, and it learns by association instead of by logic or reason. That's why you can't simply talk yourself out of irrational fears and why exposure techniques are so powerful. The more times you get scared in a crowded grocery store, the more strongly your brain will associate crowded grocery stores with danger. If you leave the grocery store because of your fear, you're telling your brain that you successfully escaped a dangerous situation—which in turn will strengthen your brain's association of crowds with danger. By contrast, the more times you are able to "survive" the crowded grocery store, the more information you are giving your brain about the crowded grocery store not actually being dangerous.

Exposure works, but it isn't easy. If a situation is only mildly unpleasant for you, exposure isn't typically necessary because you likely don't have a strong association between fear and that situation. It only works when you have a strong physiological fear reaction to something, which is often highly uncomfortable but not inherently harmful. For exposure to work, you need to be willing to experience some hard things, and you need to trust the process. This is why we've talked so much about how your brain learns to associate harmless stimuli with fear, and how your brain can *unlearn* these same associations. You can remember this when you're doing an exposure exercise and your brain starts shouting that you're in danger. You're not; it's just the old associations cropping up as you're retraining your brain to make new ones. It may also help you to know that these techniques have been repeatedly studied on thousands of individuals with anxiety, and, when done right, have been shown to be highly effective.

Because exposure can be so hard, you want to make sure you have some core coping skills down first, like slow breathing and catching yourself when you start to engage in the common thinking errors, like catastrophizing. You also want to carefully select your targets for exposure. Don't start with the scariest thing on your list of fears, but rather start from the bottom and work your way up. Later in this chapter you'll find a worksheet to help you organize your exposure plan. Finally, make sure that you take necessary safety precautions, including receiving a full physical and medical clearance and having someone you trust with you when you tackle the harder things on your list. If you regularly use fast-acting anti-anxiety medications (like Xanax or Klonopin), be aware that they could interfere with the exposure process because they block your natural fear reaction.

Before you create your exposure plan, you'll need to know about the three types of exposure you can work with, starting with imagining the thing you fear in great detail.

Imaginal Exposure

Imaginal exposure involves vividly imagining and describing the feared object, situation, or sensation. In order for imaginal exposure to be effective, make your visualization as realistic as possible. Use present-tense language when describing what you are imagining, and conjure up as much detail as possible about what you imagine would be happening around you (e.g., sights, sounds, and smells) and inside you (e.g., thoughts and emotions). Do imaginal exposures with someone you trust to support you, at least the first couple of times. You can describe the situations to them. If you do the exercise alone, it can still be helpful to describe what you are visualizing out loud. If you don't feel any fear when you talk about or imagine a feared situation or object, exposure won't work. So you want to find the situation on your list of feared alternative behaviors (see "How Scary Are Your Alternative Behaviors?" on page 81) that is scary enough that just imagining going through it gives you a physiological fear reaction (e.g., heart racing).

Imaginal exposure can also be used for confronting your "worst-case scenario" fears, like imagining that you lose control during a panic attack and start screaming uncontrollably, or imagining getting stuck in a broken elevator while panicking and having people ridicule you. However, it is not effective to use imaginal exposure to work though totally unrealistic fears like dying from a panic attack. These types of fears are more easily worked through using tools for developing more realistic thought patterns, as we discussed in chapter 4.

I once worked with a woman, whom I'll call Kendra, who avoided movie theaters and other crowded public spaces due to fears that she would have a panic attack and would not be able to escape quickly enough, and that people would laugh and point at her while she was panicking. Although she could face her fears of crowded spaces in real life (formally called in vivo exposure and discussed in more detail on page 86), we could not recreate the public ridicule that was a huge part of her worst-case scenario thinking. During the imaginal exposure exercise, Kendra described in excruciating detail the hurtful things people would say to her and the mean looks on their faces. She also talked about how much it would hurt her feelings to experience this, and described in real time the thoughts she imagined she would have (e.g., "I knew I was a total loser"). It was obvious that it felt real to her, as her voice and body shook while she described her fears of being publicly ridiculed during a panic attack. She stayed with the exercise long enough that her fear subsided while she was still engaged in the visualization of her feared scenario, thus breaking the association between the thoughts and her physiological fear response. Each time she repeated the exercise, Kendra felt less fear and was scared for shorter durations of time.

Imaginal Exposure

This exercise will give you an opportunity to practice this type of exposure. You will first write in detail about a feared scenario, and then close your eyes and try to visualize the scenario while describing, out loud and in the present tense, what you are experiencing.

1. Write out your feared scenario in as much detail as possible. Include what you imagine would be happening around you (e.g., sights, sounds, and smells) as well as what you imagine would be happening inside you (e.g., thoughts and feelings).

_____

_____

_____

_____

2. Close your eyes. Visualize the scenario in step 1 and describe, out loud and in present tense, everything that you imagine is happening around you (e.g., sights, sounds, and smells) as well as what you imagine would be happening inside you (e.g., thoughts and feelings). For example, "I see everyone laughing and my heart is pounding in my chest."

    Rate the peak of your anxiety during the exercise (on a scale of 0 to 10, with 0 representing no anxiety and 10 representing maximum anxiety): _____

Repeat the exercise until your peak anxiety rating decreases significantly.

The next type of exposure will take you into the world to confront a fearful activity or situation.

In Vivo Exposure

In vivo exposure refers to real-world confrontation of feared stimuli. Because panic disorder often involves fears surrounding activities and situations, as well as fears of specific physical sensations that signal panic or are a part of your panic experience, in vivo exposure exercises need to target both aspects. _The important thing to keep in mind is that you need to stick with the exercise long enough for your fear to subside._ As we have talked about, if you "escape" by ending the exercise prematurely because it becomes too uncomfortable or scary, you are signaling to your brain that you escaped a real danger, thus strengthening your brain's fear reaction in response to that stimuli.

You need to give yourself enough time to learn new information. You also need to repeat the experience with enough regularity that the new learning is reinforced. For example, if you jog once, despite your fears that exercise will induce panic, but then wait a few weeks to do it again, you won't give yourself enough practice for your brain to learn the new association. But if you jog multiple times a week for increasing durations of time, you will be regularly accumulating new information, like learning that being short of breath doesn't signal danger, that you can jog without inducing panic, or that even if you do experience a panic attack while jogging, it is relatively brief and something that you can manage.

When you develop your exposure plans, pay attention to the details. For instance, if one of your feared scenarios is becoming overheated while exercising and not having your anxiety medications with you, eventually you will want to expose yourself to this exact scenario. If you simply expose yourself to exercise but always have your medications with you "just in case," even if you never take it, you are still avoiding one aspect of your feared scenario. For many people, the conditions of their first panic attack set the stage for further panic to develop. Think back to your first panic attack. At some point it may be helpful to recreate this scenario.

It may also be helpful to bring someone with you when you do exposure exercises. As long as you educate your support person about the exposure process, and especially about the importance of letting your anxiety and panic peak prior to exiting the situation, they can offer an added safety net and help encourage you to stick with the exposure during the tough moments.

When you engage in intentional, systematic, and regular exposure, you will eventually learn that what you're most worried about happening is actually quite unlikely, and you will learn that what you fear the most is not nearly as bad as you imagined. You'll also learn that you can handle and survive feelings of anxiety and panic, however uncomfortable they may be.

In Vivo Situation Exposure

To do an in vivo situation exposure, start by describing the situation or activity you fear, and include any negative thoughts you associate with it. Try to counter any exaggerated or distorted thinking. Describe a specific goal for your exposure exercise (it may be a step in the direction of your full feared situation or activity), and remind yourself of the coping tools available to you. Complete the exercise. Rate your anxiety level at its peak, and repeat until your anxiety rating decreases.

Feared situation or activity:

_____

_____

Negative thoughts associated with the situation or activity (i.e., what you are most worried about happening):

_____

_____

More realistic thoughts about the situation or activity:

_____

_____

Specific goal for today (describe in detail what you plan to do and how long you plan to do it):

_____

_____

Coping skills available to me:

_____

_____

Rate the peak of your anxiety during the exposure exercise (on a scale of 0 to 10, with 0 representing no anxiety and 10 representing maximum anxiety): _____

Repeat the exercise until your peak anxiety rating decreases significantly.

In the third type of exposure, you will directly confront the bodily sensations that accompany your panic. As with the other two types of exposure activities, you will begin with some of the milder types of sensations you associate with a panic attack.

In Vivo Sensation Exposure

As we've discussed, a central feature of panic disorder is an exaggerated fear response to physiological sensations that mimic panic or that you associate with a full-blown panic attack. We have already talked about developing more realistic thoughts about what these sensations mean (e.g., that chest tightness does not necessarily signal a heart attack), and now you're ready to face the physical sensations directly, to continue to learn that they are not harmful and that you can handle the discomfort.

One reason fears of physical symptoms persist is that your body has become highly sensitive to the physical feelings that signal the beginning of a panic attack. Exposure to your feared physical sensations will make your body less conditioned to associating these sensations with panic, and thus the symptoms will become less likely to set off a full panic reaction.

Here are examples of how to induce panic symptoms and physiological sensations:

- Breathlessness or smothering sensations

  * Hyperventilate
  * Hold your breath
  * Breathe through a narrow straw or into a paper bag

- Rapid heart rate

  * Run up stairs
  * Do jumping jacks

- Choking sensation

  * Place a tongue depressor on the back of your tongue
  * Place your toothbrush in the back of your mouth

- Dry mouth

  * Breathe with your mouth open for a few moments
  * Eat dry saltine crackers without water

- Dizziness or feeling faint

  * Spin in a circle
  * Shake your head rapidly

- Temperature change

  * Drive with the heat on
  * Wear multiple layers of warm clothing

This next exercise will let you practice facing the physical symptoms that you associate with panic.

In Vivo Symptom Exposure

Before you begin, decide how you are going to induce or provoke the panic sensations that are more tolerable for you, but still distressing, and decide how long you are going to engage in the exercise. Begin the exercise in a location that is safe and comfortable. When you're ready, do the exercise for a minimum of 30 seconds, or until you first notice symptoms. Remember that it's helpful to have a trusted friend or family member nearby. Try to continue beyond the point of simply noticing symptoms, and eventually produce the symptoms as strongly as possible. It will be natural to do the exercises mildly or with hesitation at first. Recognize this partial effort as a form of avoidance and eventually work up to the full expression of the sensation.

Eventually, you will work your way up to the most unpleasant and/or most frightening symptoms.

What I am going to do:

_____

How long I am going to do it:

_____

Negative thoughts associated with the symptom (i.e., what you are most worried about happening):

_____

Rate the peak of your anxiety during the exercise (on a scale of 0 to 10, with 0 representing no anxiety and 10 representing maximum anxiety): _____

Repeat the exercise until your peak anxiety rating decreases significantly. With experience of each of the three types of exposure under your belt, and your list of feared situations in ranked order (see "How Scary Are Your Alternative Behaviors?" on page 81), you can now put this all together and develop your own exposure plan. The next worksheet will guide you through this part of the process.

Exposure Hierarchy

Review your worksheets on avoidance and alternative behaviors. Select ten situations or sensations that you predict will induce the lowest levels of anxiety. Work your way up the list only after you have experienced a significant reduction in fear related to those situations or sensations.

Expected Level of Anxiety	Feared Situation, Activity, or Sensation	Exposure Plan: (Imaginal, In Vivo Situation or Activity, In Vivo Sensation Induction)
100		
90		
80		
70		
60		
50		
40		
30		
20		
10		

Recognizing the gains you're making and identifying issues for renewed focus will help you progress. Remember that exposure techniques have been shown to be highly effective when properly applied.

Avoidance and Exposure Progress Record

Over the next 10 weeks, use the log below to track how often you engage in avoidance behaviors versus how often you act courageously by engaging in behavior that is not driven by avoidance. If you do not see a reduction in avoidance behaviors over time, you may need to increase your alternative behaviors and formal exposure exercises. Though this log tracks a week at a time, you may find it helpful to track these efforts each day so your weekly counts are accurate.

	Avoidance Behaviors (#)	Use of Safety Objects or Excessive Safety Measures (#)	Alternatives to Avoidance/ Acts of Courage (#)	Exposure Exercises (#)

Week 1: _____

Week 2: _____

Week 3: _____

Week 4: _____

Week 5: _____

Week 6: _____

Week 7: _____

Week 8: _____

Week 9: _____

Week 10: _____

Key Takeaways

In this chapter we learned how easy it is to get caught in the trap of avoiding what scares us, but that in the long run avoidance only serves to increase our anxiety. After completing this chapter, you should have a good understanding of:

- What you are avoiding and why.

- How avoidance increases fear by telling your brain that false alarms are real danger.

- How exposure is the best way to lessen your fear response because it teaches your brain new information about the feared scenarios or sensations.

- The importance of continuing with an exposure exercise until fear subsides.

- The differences between imaginal and in vivo exposures.

- The importance of graduated exposure (i.e., starting with less feared scenarios and working your way up to more feared scenarios).

CHAPTER SIX:

Looking Ahead

Congratulations! You've done a lot of work and are hopefully already seeing the benefits in reduced intensity of your panic symptoms and fewer panic attacks. Be aware that greatly reduced frequency, or even elimination, of attacks *today* doesn't guarantee that panic is gone from your life forever. If you experience increased stress or a major life change, it's fairly likely that your panic attacks could return to previous levels, or worsen. In addition to managing your stress levels, it will be crucial that you remain active and engaged with the coping and self-care strategies that you have found worked best for you so far. This will help protect against future attacks and help you bounce back more quickly (instead of spiraling) if your symptoms reoccur down the line.

In this final section of the book, we'll review how far you've come, the goals you've accomplished, and the important (and challenging) changes you've already made. We will also develop a solid long-term plan for managing your anxiety going forward.

Progress Review

Let's take a moment to check in on the progress you have made so far. First, simply reflect on how you're doing and where you are with your panic symptoms. Next, take a look at your panic attack progress records for some data. If you haven't been keeping logs, it's never too late to start.

Our memories are highly susceptible to distortion based on things like current mood and emotional states. We are more likely to remember things that went well when we're feeling good, and more likely to remember things that went wrong when we are feeling discouraged or down. That's why it's so important to keep track of how things are actually going, in real time. When evaluating your progress, try to take a bird's-eye view. Even if you had a recent week with a higher than average number of panic attacks, what does the bigger picture look like? Overall, has the number of panic attacks you experience each week gone down? How about the severity? Are your symptoms as intense as they were when you began this program? Are you using your coping skills? How often are you engaging in slow breathing techniques, or catching negative or exaggerated thought patterns? Checking in on your progress regularly can help you be realistic about how you are progressing and can help you decide where to focus your energies.

Progress Check

Take a moment to review your progress in managing your panic symptoms and strengthening your coping skills.

Wherever you see progress, take a moment to appreciate that your hard work has produced this beneficial effect on your life. Learning and implementing strategies to deal with (and reduce) experiences of panic doesn't happen overnight. Come back in the future and do this exercise again.

Have you noticed improvements in regard to the frequency of your panic symptoms?

1   2   3   4   5   6   7   8   9   10

Not at all   A little   Moderately   A lot   Significantly

Have you noticed improvements in regard to the severity of your panic symptoms?

1   2   3   4   5   6   7   8   9   10

Not at all   A little   Moderately   A lot   Significantly

Have you noticed improvements in regard to your level of anxiety about your panic symptoms?

1   2   3   4   5   6   7   8   9   10

Not at all   A little   Moderately   A lot   Significantly

Have you noticed improvements in regard to your negative thought patterns, including jumping to conclusions or catastrophizing?

1   2   3   4   5   6   7   8   9   10

Not at all   A little   Moderately   A lot   Significantly

Have you noticed a reduction in your level of situation or activity avoidance?

1   2   3   4   5   6   7   8   9   10

Not at all   A little   Moderately   A lot   Significantly

Practice, Practice, Practice

It's often the hard things in our lives that motivate us to make the biggest changes. If your panic didn't really bother you, you would have been less likely to pick up this book and try to make changes. Hopefully things are going better for you now than they were when you started this journey. But don't wait for things to get bad again to start practicing these skills or revisiting the exercises. The more consistently you use the tools you learned in this workbook, the more readily available they will be for you when you really need them.

It will take some discipline to keep practicing when things are going better and some of the urgency has faded. The next exercise will help you set up a plan for continuing to practice your new skills in an ongoing way. It will also be helpful to set some future reminders for yourself. Go to your calendar and write a brief note to yourself at 3-, 6-, 9-, and 12-month intervals (or whatever time frame makes the most sense for you) to check in with your mental health and your panic symptoms. When those dates roll around, ask yourself if you are still actively using your coping skills and maintaining daily wellness habits. If so, great! If not, it would be a good time to pick up this book again and get back on track.

Planning for Practicing Exercises

Use the following log to keep you on track with practicing your coping skills. You can fill out the log ahead of time and use it for planning purposes (e.g., "Monday I will work on breathing skills"), or you can use the log to record which skills you worked on and to track your practice. Or, develop a recording system that works for you (e.g., "X" or "□" for planned practice and "✔" for a completed practice exercise).

Week of: _____	Practice breathing skills	Practice thinking skills	Face feared situation(s)	Face feared sensations/ panic symptoms	Focus on developing healthy habits	Other: _____
Monday						
Tuesday						
Wednesday						
Thursday						
Friday						
Saturday						
Sunday						

Targeting Your Biggest Challenges

Looking back, what were the biggest challenges you faced in this workbook? Were there particular avoidance behaviors that were hard to eliminate? Are there activities or places that still trigger panic? Even if you are doing much better, try to develop a mind-set of continuous growth, and be honest with yourself about whether or not there are still things you are avoiding. If you continue to face the things that make you anxious, you will continue to get stronger and your anxiety will continue to shrink. In contrast, if you are still avoiding something that is making you anxious, this avoidance behavior could feed your anxiety and become a stumbling block in the future.

What I Have Learned from My Biggest Challenges

Reflect back on the biggest challenges you have faced thus far. What were they? What did you do to try to overcome those challenges? What worked? What can you do now to continue to face these challenges head-on?

_____

_____

_____

_____

_____

_____

_____

_____

What I Want to Work on Next

What goal are you working on now? Use this worksheet to identify the primary short- and long-term goals that you want to focus on now. Your short-term goal should help you work toward your long-term goal.

My next goal:

_____

_____

_____

The reason I want to work on this goal is:

_____

_____

_____

This goal will help me reach my long-term goal, which is:

_____

_____

_____

Finding What Works for You

Another benefit of the documentation and record keeping you have done throughout the workbook is that you can figure out what works best for you. Review your panic attack progress records again. Pay especially close attention to the weeks when the number or severity of panic attacks you experienced was particularly high or low. What was going on? This type of analysis can provide you with important information about what works best for *you*.

For instance, if you notice that a week when your panic attacks were particularly low coincided with a time period during which you'd gotten plenty of sleep, exercised regularly, were socially engaged, and did brief daily meditations, this gives you a lot of clues as to which strategies helped reduce your panic. On the other hand, if you notice that a week with particularly severe panic was preceded by a week during which your stress increased and you stopped actively practicing your thinking and reframing skills, that is valuable to know. Sometimes periods that bring a challenging increase in symptoms offer the silver lining of lots of good information about what is and isn't working for you.

FINDING MORE SUPPORT

As you continue on your healing journey, don't hesitate to reach out for help. A support network can include friends and family as well as in-person or online support groups, which are sometimes free of cost, and individual or group therapy (see the Resources section on page 119 for structured support options).

It can also be helpful to make the most of the support that you have in your existing network of friends, family, and loved ones. Asking for what you need, and being open to receiving that support, is a courageous act, but you already know how to do hard things. Research shows that involving other people in your recovery process facilitates further growth and improvement. It is particularly important that at least some of the people, and especially those closest to you, have a good understanding of panic disorder. If the people around you are unaware of the nature of panic disorder and the factors that increase symptoms, they may inadvertently reinforce your fears and avoidance, which could increase your symptoms. On the flip side, you do not want loved ones to be overly harsh or critical of you when your behavior is being driven by your symptoms. The more educated the people around you are about panic disorder, the more helpful they will be.

It will also be helpful for your support team to learn a little bit about the mechanisms that help reduce fear and panic, like the breathing, relaxation, and cognitive skills we've discussed throughout the workbook. This will be particularly important for anyone who is supporting you with some of your exposure exercises. You may also want to take the time to brainstorm with this person ways that they may be inadvertently reinforcing your fear and avoidance, so you can develop a plan of corrective action.

Finally, your support network can also provide you with an extra set of eyes to help you catch increases in your avoidance behavior, or times when you are becoming less active with your coping skills and basic health habits. Receiving effective support comes down to asking for help and being clear about what would be most helpful for you.

Staying on Track

If you have access to professional mental health services, that is a great way to continue to learn how to manage and reduce your panic. If you don't have access, or aren't interested at this point in seeking professional support, you can still plan for a panic-free future by keeping up your practice exercises, maintaining awareness of the factors that exacerbate your panic, and being proactive about your overall physical health. As we've discussed, you can do a lot to maximize the effectiveness of whatever support you do have. It may also be helpful to loop in your usual health care providers (like a family doctor or nurse practitioner) on your experiences with panic, and tell them what you're doing to manage it. They may be able to provide you with additional resources, like medication support (if applicable) or access to free or low-cost resources.

Maintaining progress, staying on track, and navigating bumps in the road will look different for everyone. One person might successfully eliminate their panic attacks for years, only to experience a dramatic return of symptoms when an unfamiliar life event comes up, like a child's graduation that requires both air travel and sitting for hours in an overcrowded auditorium. Someone else may never fully eliminate their panic symptoms, but by developing long-lasting wellness habits and strong coping skills, they succeed in steadily reducing the severity of their anxiety and live a full life. You may have been able to fully resolve your panic-related catastrophic thinking, only to have it reappear again in the face of a new physiological symptom. The road to progress may not be straight, but as long as you return to the core skills outlined in this workbook you will be able to get back on track.

Whatever road you're on, if you are willing to do the work, things will get better. As Virgin Group founder Richard Branson once said, "Every success story is a tale of constant adaption, revision, and change." Don't stop here. Continue to adapt, revise, and change your story for the better. All this hard work isn't just about reducing your panic symptoms. It's also about taking back your life and living in a way that honors what matters most to you.

Blank Worksheets

Panic Log

Date:_____ Time started:_____ Time ended:_____

Situation: _____

Did you expect this panic attack? Yes / No

What symptoms did you experience? Circle the symptoms that were the most distressing to you.

- ❑ Palpitations, pounding heart, or accelerated heart rate
- ❑ Sweating
- ❑ Trembling or shaking
- ❑ Sensations of shortness of breath or smothering
- ❑ Feelings of choking
- ❑ Chest pain or discomfort
- ❑ Nausea or abdominal distress
- ❑ Feeling dizzy, unsteady, lightheaded, or faint
- ❑ Chills or heat sensations
- ❑ Paresthesia (numbness or tingling sensations)
- ❑ Derealization (feelings of unreality)
- ❑ Depersonalization (feeling detached from yourself)
- ❑ Fear of losing control or "going crazy"
- ❑ Fear of dying
- ❑ Other: _____

Think about the period before the attack began. What were you thinking and doing?

Thoughts: _____

_____

Behaviors:_____

_____

What was your level of discomfort-on a scale of 1 to 10, 1 (minimal) to 10 (extreme)? _____

Keeping notes about your experiences and learning to understand and detect your thinking errors can provide useful information. Now that you've identified your thinking errors and come up with a few alternative possibilities, it's time to put them to the test.

Testing Your Theories in Real Life

Pick a belief or hypothesis to test in real life, following the approach described on page 57 in the example of having a panic attack in public. After testing it out, use the following questions to reflect upon what you learned in your first round of hypothesis testing.

What belief/hypothesis did you test?

_____

_____

_____

What was your worst fear related to this belief?

_____

_____

_____

How accurate was your belief?

_____

_____

_____

What did you learn from this experience?

_____

_____

_____

How has this new information modified your prior belief/hypothesis?

_____

_____

_____

Just as in the earlier example, you may find yourself thinking of some way to rationalize the experience so you can hang on to your belief. If this happens, test it again, as many times as it takes to recognize a shift in your belief.

Reframing Your Thinking Errors

Use the table below to help you identify and correct your typical thinking errors. If you aren't able to catch your irrational thoughts right away, just start with thoughts that cause you to feel upset and then determine if each thought is exaggerated or extreme.

Remember that the common thinking errors are:

- Catastrophizing

- Jumping to conclusions or predicting the future

- Tunnel vision

- Emotional reasoning

- Overgeneralization

Distressing thought	What type of thinking error is this?	Alternative explanations: What is a more balanced/realistic way of thinking about this?

Developing Realistic Odds

The goal of this exercise is to help you become more realistic in your thinking about panic. Start with one of your negative beliefs about panic sensations and then work through other possible explanations for that sensation.

List one of your negative beliefs about a panic sensation: _____
_____

Fill in the circles in this exercise like a pie chart, with the largest piece of the pie representing the most likely scenario.

The first circle represents your initial beliefs, or the beliefs you have during panic. So, if you are 100 percent sure that the discomfort in your chest during panic signals that you're having a heart attack, the circle will not be divided, and you will simply write "heart attack" in the middle. If you are 90 percent sure you are having a heart attack, but recognize that there is a 10 percent chance your chest pain is due to anxious thoughts, divide the pie accordingly. Now take the negative belief you listed earlier and divide the pie.

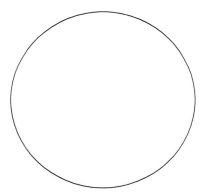

Next, think through all the possible alternative scenarios. What is the evidence for or against each of these possibilities? Complete the circle again, this time trying to be as realistic as possible and including your alternative scenarios.

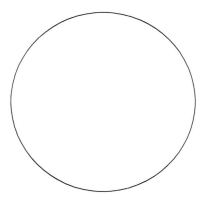

Panic Attack Progress Record

Panic Attacks (#)	Week 1 Date: ___	Week 2 Date: ___	Week 3 Date: ___	Week 4 Date: ___	Week 5 Date: ___	Week 6 Date: ___	Week 7 Date: ___	Week 8 Date: ___
10								
9								
8								
7								
6								
5								
4								
3								
2								
1								
0								

Imaginal Exposure

This exercise will give you an opportunity to practice this type of exposure. You will first write in detail about a feared scenario, and then close your eyes and try to visualize the scenario while describing, out loud and in the present tense, what you are experiencing.

1. Write out your feared scenario in as much detail as possible. Include what you imagine would be happening around you (e.g., sights, sounds, and smells) as well as what you imagine would be happening inside you (e.g., thoughts and feelings).

_____

_____

_____

_____

2. Close your eyes. Visualize the scenario in step 1 and describe, out loud and in present tense, everything that you imagine is happening around you (e.g., sights, sounds, and smells) as well as what you imagine would be happening inside you (e.g., thoughts and feelings). For example, "I see everyone laughing and my heart is pounding in my chest."

   Rate the peak of your anxiety during the exercise (on a scale of 0 to 10, with 0 representing no anxiety and 10 representing maximum anxiety): _____

Repeat the exercise until your peak anxiety rating decreases significantly.

The next type of exposure will take you into the world to confront a fearful activity or situation.

In Vivo Situation Exposure

To do an in vivo situation exposure, start by describing the situation or activity you fear, and include any negative thoughts you associate with it. Try to counter any exaggerated or distorted thinking. Describe a specific goal for your exposure exercise (it may be a step in the direction of your full feared situation or activity), and remind yourself of the coping tools available to you. Complete the exercise. Rate your anxiety level at its peak, and repeat until your anxiety rating decreases.

Feared situation or activity:

_____

_____

Negative thoughts associated with the situation or activity (i.e., what you are most worried about happening):

_____

_____

More realistic thoughts about the situation or activity:

_____

_____

Specific goal for today (describe in detail what you plan to do and how long you plan to do it):

_____

_____

Coping skills available to me:

_____

_____

Rate the peak of your anxiety during the exposure exercise (on a scale of 0 to 10, with 0 representing no anxiety and 10 representing maximum anxiety): _____

Repeat the exercise until your peak anxiety rating decreases significantly.

In the third type of exposure, you will directly confront the bodily sensations that accompany your panic. As with the other two types of exposure activities, you will begin with some of the milder types of sensations you associate with a panic attack.

In Vivo Sensation Exposure

As we've discussed, a central feature of panic disorder is an exaggerated fear response to physiological sensations that mimic panic or that you associate with a full-blown panic attack. We have already talked about developing more realistic thoughts about what these sensations mean (e.g., that chest tightness does not necessarily signal a heart attack), and now you're ready to face the physical sensations directly, to continue to learn that they are not harmful and that you can handle the discomfort.

One reason fears of physical symptoms persist is that your body has become highly sensitive to the physical feelings that signal the beginning of a panic attack. Exposure to your feared physical sensations will make your body less conditioned to associating these sensations with panic, and thus the symptoms will become less likely to set off a full panic reaction.

Here are examples of how to induce panic symptoms and physiological sensations:

- Breathlessness or smothering sensations
  * Hyperventilate
  * Hold your breath
  * Breathe through a narrow straw or into a paper bag

- Rapid heart rate
  * Run up stairs
  * Do jumping jacks

- Choking sensation
  * Place a tongue depressor on the back of your tongue
  * Place your toothbrush in the back of your mouth

- Dry mouth
  * Breathe with your mouth open for a few moments
  * Eat dry saltine crackers without water

In Vivo Symptom Exposure

Before you begin, decide how you are going to induce or provoke the panic sensations that are more tolerable for you, but still distressing, and decide how long you are going to engage in the exercise. Begin the exercise in a location that is safe and comfortable. When you're ready, do the exercise for a minimum of 30 seconds, or until you first notice symptoms. Remember that it's helpful to have a trusted friend or family member nearby. Try to continue beyond the point of simply noticing symptoms, and eventually produce the symptoms as strongly as possible. It will be natural to do the exercises mildly or with hesitation at first. Recognize this partial effort as a form of avoidance and eventually work up to the full expression of the sensation.

Eventually, you will work your way up to the most unpleasant and/or most frightening symptoms.

What I am going to do:

_____

How long I am going to do it:

_____

Negative thoughts associated with the symptom (i.e., what you are most worried about happening):

_____

Rate the peak of your anxiety during the exercise (on a scale of 0 to 10, with 0 representing no anxiety and 10 representing maximum anxiety): _____

Repeat the exercise until your peak anxiety rating decreases significantly. With experience of each of the three types of exposure under your belt, and your list of feared situations in ranked order (see "How Scary Are Your Alternative Behaviors?" on page 81), you can now put this all together and develop your own exposure plan. The next worksheet will guide you through this part of the process.

Avoidance and Exposure Progress Record

Over the next 10 weeks, use the log below to track how often you engage in avoidance behaviors versus how often you act courageously by engaging in behavior that is not driven by avoidance. If you do not see a reduction in avoidance behaviors over time, you may need to increase your alternative behaviors and formal exposure exercises. Though this log tracks a week at a time, you may find it helpful to track these efforts each day so your weekly counts are accurate.

	Avoidance Behaviors (#)	Use of Safety Objects or Excessive Safety Measures (#)	Alternatives to Avoidance/ Acts of Courage (#)	Exposure Exercises (#)
Week 1: _____				
Week 2: _____				
Week 3: _____				
Week 4: _____				
Week 5: _____				
Week 6: _____				
Week 7: _____				
Week 8: _____				
Week 9: _____				
Week 10: _____				

Planning for Practicing Exercises

Week of: _____	Practice breathing skills	Practice thinking skills	Face feared situation(s)	Face feared sensations/ panic symptoms	Focus on developing healthy habits	Other: _____
Monday						
Tuesday						
Wednes-day						
Thursday						
Friday						
Saturday						
Sunday						

Resources

Anxiety and Depression Association of America: https://www.adaa.org
This site provides information about anxiety, as well as online support groups.

The Anxiety Network: https://www.anxietynetwork.com
This site provides information about anxiety and anxiety disorders, as well as treatment tools and links to further resources.

Fast Calm app
This free app from Apple uses visual exercises and breathing exercises to help you calm down and control your breathing during times of panic and anxiety.

Capt. Ron's Fearless Flight: https://www.fearlessflight.com
This program was developed for individuals with a fear of flying, but it can also be helpful for people who are scared of flying due to panic symptoms. The program offers actual flights in select cities and online flight simulations for exposure exercises.

Mental Health America: http://www.mentalhealthamerica.net
Mental Health America offers many resources for your mental health including screening tools, a crisis line, and a support group search tool.

National Alliance of Mental Illness: https://www.nami.org/Learn-More /Mental-Health-Conditions/Anxiety-Disorders/Support
Local chapters provide education and support groups for individuals with anxiety disorders, as well as resources for families and friends of people experiencing anxiety disorders.

Psychology Today: https://www.psychologytoday.com/us
Psychology Today offers many brief articles on various mental health topics, as well as a national database of therapists and support groups.

Stop Panic and Anxiety Self-Help app
This free app, available on Android, uses CBT techniques to help you manage your panic symptoms, and includes an anxiety diary.

UCLA Mindful Awareness Research Center: http://marc.ucla.edu
The UCLA Mindful Awareness Research Center offers a library of free audio-guided meditations, as well as other resources related to mindfulness.

References

Anderson, E., and G. Shivakumar. "Effects of Exercise and Physical Activity on Anxiety." *Frontiers in Psychiatry* 4.27 (2013). doi:10.3389/fpsyt.2013.00027.

Barlow, David H., and Michelle G. Craske. *Mastery of Your Anxiety and Panic.* New York: Oxford University Press, 2007.

Birchall, H., S. Brandon, and N. Taub. "Panic in a General Practice Population: Prevalence, Psychiatric Comorbidity and Associated Disability. *Social Psychiatry and Psychiatric Epidemiology: The International Journal for Research in Social and Genetic Epidemiology and Mental Health Services* 35, no. 6 (2000): 235–241.

Bischoff, S., et al. "Running for Extinction? Aerobic Exercise as an Augmentation of Exposure Therapy in Panic Disorder with Agoraphobia." *Journal of Psychiatric Research* 101 (2018): 34–41.

Brown, Brené. *Daring Greatly: How the Courage to Be Vulnerable Transforms the Way We Live, Love, Parent, and Lead.* New York: Gotham Books, 2012.

Carbonell, David. *Panic Attacks Workbook: A Guided Program for Beating the Panic Trick.* Berkeley, CA: Ulysses Press, 2004.

Carpenter, J.K., L.A. Andrews, S.M. Witcraft, M.B. Powers, J.A.J. Smits, and S.G. Hofmann, S.G. (2018). "Cognitive Behavioral Therapy for Anxiety and Related Disorders: A Meta-Analysis of Randomized Placebo-Controlled Trials. *Depression and Anxiety* 35, no. 6 (2018): 502–514.

Clark, David A., and Aaron T. Beck. *The Anxiety and Worry Workbook: The Cognitive Behavioral Solution.* New York: The Guilford Press, 2012.

de Jonge, P., et al. "Cross-National Epidemiology of Panic Disorder and Panic Attacks in the World Mental Health Surveys." *Depression and Anxiety* 33, no. 12 (2016): 1155–1177.

Erhardt, A., et al. "Regulation of the Hypothalamic-Pituitary-Adrenocortical System in Patients with Panic Disorder. *Neuropsychopharmacology*, 31, no. 11 (2006): 2515–2522.

Foldes-Busque, G., I. Denis, J. Poitras, R.P. Fleet, P.M. Archambault, and C.E. Dionne. "The Revised-Panic Screening Score for Emergency Department Patients with Noncardiac Chest Pain." *Health Psychology*, 37, no. 9 (2018): 828–838.

Gordon, T., and J. Borushok. *The ACT Approach: A Comprehensive Guide for Acceptance and Commitment Therapy.* Eau Claire, WI: PESI Publishing and Media, 2017.

Gratz, K.L., M.T. Tull, and A.W. Wagner. "Applying DBT Mindfulness Skills to the Treatment of Clients with Anxiety Disorders." In *Series in Anxiety and Related Disorders: Acceptance and Mindfulness-Based Approaches to Anxiety*, edited by Susan M. Orsillo and Lizbeth Roemer. Boston: Springer, 2005.

Hawley, L.L., J. Rogojanski, V. Vorstenbosch, L.C. Quilty, J.M. Laposa, and N.A. Rector. "The Structure, Correlates, and Treatment Related Changes of Mindfulness Facets Across the Anxiety Disorders and Obsessive Compulsive Disorder." *Journal of Anxiety Disorders* 49 (2017): 65–75.

Kabat-Zinn, J., et al. "Effectiveness of a Meditation-Based Stress Reduction Program in the Treatment of Anxiety Disorders." In *Mindfulness: Clinical Applications of Mindfulness and Acceptance: Specific Interventions for Psychiatric, Behavioral, and Physical Health Conditions*, Vol. III. edited by B.A. Gaudiano, 188–204. New York: Routledge/Taylor & Francis Group, 2017.

Kessler, R.C., W.T. Chiu, R. Jin, A.M. Ruscio, K. Shear, and E.E. Walters. "The Epidemiology of Panic Attacks, Panic Disorder, and Agoraphobia in the National Comorbidity Survey Replication." *Archives of General Psychiatry* 63, no. 4 (2006): 415–424.

Kiecolt-Glaser, J.K., M.A. Belury, R. Andridge, W.B. Malarkey, and R. Glaser. "Omega-3 Supplementation Lowers Inflammation and Anxiety in Medical Students: A Randomized Controlled Trial." *Brain Behavior and Immunity* 25(8) (2011):1725–1734.

Neufang, S., et al. "Cognitive-Behavioral Therapy Effects on Alerting Network Activity and Effective Connectivity in Panic Disorder. *European Archives of Psychiatry and Clinical Neuroscience* (2018): 1–12. doi:10.1007/s00406-018-0945-8.

Orsillo, Susan M., and Lizbeth Roemer. *The Mindful Way Through Anxiety*. New York: The Guilford Press, 2011.

Otto, Michael, and Jasper A.J. Smits. *Exercise for Mood and Anxiety: Proven Strategies for Overcoming Depression and Enhancing Well-Being*. New York: Oxford University Press, 2011.

Pompoli, A., T.A. Furukawa, O. Efthimiou, H. Imai, A. Tajika, and G. Salanti. "Dismantling Cognitive-Behaviour Therapy for Panic Disorder: A Systematic Review and Component Network Meta-Analysis." *Psychological Medicine* 48, no. 12 (2018): 1945–1953.

Pompoli, A., T.A. Furukawa, H. Imai, A. Tajika, O. Efthimiou, and G. Salanti. "Psychological Therapies for Panic Disorder with or without Agoraphobia in Adults: A Network Meta-Analysis." *Cochrane Database of Systematic Reviews* 4 (2016). doi:10.1002/14651858 .CD011004.pub2.

Ritzert, T., J.P. Forsyth, S.C. Sheppard, J.F. Boswell, C.R. Berghoff, and G.H. Eifert. "Evaluating the Effectiveness of ACT for Anxiety Disorders in a Self-Help Context: Outcomes from a Randomized Wait-List Controlled Trial." *Behavior Therapy* 47 (2016): 444–459.

Sartori, S.B., N. Whittle, A. Hetzenauer, and N. Singewald. "Magnesium Deficiency Induces Anxiety and HPA Axis Dysregulation: Modulation by Therapeutic Drug Treatment." *Neuropharmacology* 62, no. 1 (2012): 304–312.

Strauss, A.Y., Y. Kivity, and J.D. Huppert. "Emotion Regulation Strategies in Cognitive Behavioral Therapy for Panic Disorder." *Behavior Therapy* 50, no. 3 (2018): 659–671.

Torabi, M., M. Kesmati, H.E. Harooni, and H.N. Varzi. "Effects of Nano and Conventional Zinc Oxide on Anxiety-like Behavior in Male Rats." *Indian Journal of Pharmacology* 45, no. 5 (2013): 508–512.

Index

Acknowledgments

A huge thank you to my friends and family, who serve as my constant cheerleaders and sources of inspiration. I am also deeply grateful for mentors, past and present, who have played a significant role in my development as a psychologist and made me a better person, especially Jerusha Detweiler-Bedell, Ph.D., Anne Brodsky, Ph.D., and David Glassmire, Ph.D. Finally, a special thanks to my editor, Camille Hayes, for making me a better writer and for her passion for making mental health treatment accessible.

About the Author

Elena Welsh, Ph.D., is a licensed clinical psychologist located in Los Angeles, California. Dr. Welsh received her doctorate from the University of Maryland, Baltimore County, and completed advanced clinical training through a postdoctoral fellowship at Gateways Hospital and Mental Health Center in Los Angeles. Dr. Welsh has worked with folks with anxiety disorders from all walks of life, in a variety of settings. She has published articles in various medical and research journals and is the author of *Trauma Survivors' Strategies for Healing: A Workbook to Help You Grow, Rebuild, and Take Back Your Life* and *Getting to Good: A Guided Journal*. Dr. Welsh has also served as an adjunct faculty member at various universities in Los Angeles.